Thriving in a Complex World
LIFE

Thriving in a Complex World
LIFE

By Ralph Ennis, Rebecca Goldstone, Judy Gomoll, Dennis Stokes, Christine Weddle

BE TRANSFORMED

NavPress is the publishing ministry of The Navigators, an international Christian organization and leader in personal spiritual development. NavPress is committed to helping people grow spiritually and enjoy lives of meaning and hope through personal and group resources that are biblically rooted, culturally relevant, and highly practical.

For a free catalog go to www.NavPress.com
or call 1.800.366.7788 in the United States or 1.800.839.4769 in Canada.

© 2008 by The Navigators

All rights reserved. No part of this publication may be reproduced in any form without written permission from NavPress, P.O. Box 35001, Colorado Springs, CO 80935. www.navpress.com

NAVPRESS and the NAVPRESS logo are registered trademarks of NavPress. Absence of ® in connection with marks of NavPress or other parties does not indicate an absence of registration of those marks.

ISBN-13: 978-1-60006-260-5
ISBN-10: 1-60006-260-1

Cover Design by The DesignWorks Group, Jason Gabbert, www.thedesignworksgroup.com

Consultation: Debbie Entsminger, Sara Wevodau, Dr. Christopher Morton

Some of the anecdotal illustrations in this book are true to life and are included with the permission of the persons involved. All other illustrations are composites of real situations, and any resemblance to people living or dead is coincidental.

Unless otherwise identified, all Scripture quotations in this publication are taken from the *HOLY BIBLE: NEW INTERNATIONAL VERSION*® (NIV®). Copyright © 1973, 1978, 1984 by International Bible Society. Used by permission of Zondervan Publishing House. All rights reserved. Other versions used include: *THE MESSAGE* (MSG). Copyright © 1993, 1994, 1995, 1996, 2000, 2001, 2002, 2005. Used by permission of NavPress Publishing Group; the *Holy Bible, New Living Translation* (NLT), copyright © 1996, 2004. Used by permission of Tyndale House Publishers, Inc., Carol Stream, Illinois 60188. All rights reserved; the *Amplified Bible* (AMP), © The Lockman Foundation 1954, 1958, 1962, 1964, 1965, 1987; the *New American Standard Bible* (NASB), © The Lockman Foundation 1960, 1962, 1963, 1968, 1971, 1972, 1973, 1975, 1977, 1995; and *The Living Bible* (TLB), Copyright © 1971, used by permission of Tyndale House Publishers, Inc., Wheaton, IL 60189, all rights reserved.

Printed in China

1 2 3 4 5 6 7 8 / 12 11 10 09 08

Contents

Introduction	7
Chapter Flow	7
Guidelines for Small Groups	9
Chapter 1 Time	13
Chapter 2 Money	31
Chapter 3 Beauty and Pleasure	49
Chapter 4 My Body	65
Chapter 5 Work	81
Chapter 6 Decisions and Commitments	99
Chapter 7 Authority	115
Chapter 8 Church	129
Chapter 9 Global Issues	149
Chapter 10 Lifetime Journey	165
Celebrating Your Group	183
Why Memorize Scripture?	185
Connect Series Overview	189
About the Authors	190

INTRODUCTION

In case this is your first study in the CONNECT series — or even if you've journeyed through other studies before you picked up this one — this overview may help you connect some dots. *GOD: Connecting with His Outrageous Love* is about receiving God's love and loving Him in response. *IDENTITY: Becoming Who God Says I Am* and *SOUL: Embracing My Sexuality and Emotions* are about discovering who God says we are and learning to live out of that true identity. *RELATIONSHIPS: Bringing Jesus into My World* is about loving people — all kinds of people. Because if we're loving God and ourselves, then loving people will happen naturally. This study is about living well with Jesus.

CHAPTER FLOW

Think of your time spent in each chapter as a mini-journey — an exploratory trip on your way toward authentic spiritual transformation. Most chapters in this study have the following sections where you'll "pause" your heart and mind along the way.

A SHORT STORY

Each is based on real-life experiences.

PAUSE 1: EXPLORING WHAT GOD SAYS

This section encourages you to look at the Bible to see what God said. We'll include most of the verses for you, from a variety of Bible translations. But nothing beats reading your own Bible to make you comfortable in God's Word. You'll be reading the *New International Version*, unless we say otherwise. Sometimes we use *The Message* (MSG), the *New Living Translation* (NLT), the *New American Standard Bible* (NASB), *The Living Bible* (TLB), or *The Amplified Bible* (AMP). As you move from chapter to chapter, you'll gradually try different approaches to studying, processing, and applying these passages.

PAUSE 2: EXPLORING YOUR REALITY

Our information-driven society makes it easy to walk away from profound truth without considering what it really says about us. This section will guide you as you try to see yourself from God's perspective and explore what it would take for you to become more like Jesus.

PAUSE 3: COMING ALIVE TO GOD AND OTHERS

Our "what's-in-it-for-me?" culture often promotes self-centeredness and shallowness in our relationships. This section will help you examine biblical principles in order to develop patterns of knowing and relating — to Him and to others — with authenticity, honesty, humility, and love.

PAUSE 4: JOURNEYING FORWARD

Being connected with Jesus as your default lifestyle means learning to trust Him with what's true about you — all the way, every day. This section invites you to process and write out what you are learning as you live in Him, as well as what you are doing with what you are learning.

DIGGING DEEPER

Like the photo album you make after a trip, in this optional section you can pause to recap and process the highlights of your experience so far. We'll give you a few "extras" if you want to explore and experience the topic of the chapter more deeply.

IMAGES

In each chapter we've included pictures and artwork to help you reflect on the topics. They are there to stimulate your imagination and heart when words fall short. Take time to gaze at the images and place yourself within these visual stories. If a photo disturbs you, that's okay; try to figure out why.

YOUR JOURNEY THROUGH EACH CHAPTER

For each chapter, expect to devote about an hour to personal preparation — more if you choose to do the optional Digging Deeper section. So pace yourself. You might try working a little at a time on a chapter — say, one section a day or twenty minutes a day — or a longer time of concentrated reflection. After a few chapters you'll find a rhythm that fits you.

GETTING YOU STARTED

To get the most from your study, we encourage you to do three simple things:

1. Read the verses meditatively, inviting the Holy Spirit to help you unpack what He wants you to understand from each verse. We've printed most passages from the *New International Version* (NIV), but occasionally quote from other translations for a fresh rendering. You may want to use your own Bible for any or all verses in this study.
2. Mark the verses to help you engage as you read. Be creative! Underline, draw circles or arrows ⟶, highlight, use colored pencils — whatever will help you process as you go.
3. Pray throughout your study, not just when you see a prayer-oriented question. Ask the Lord to shed light on what you're studying and help you connect what you read to the realities in your life.

GUIDELINES FOR SMALL GROUPS

1. Confidentiality: Do not repeat anything said or heard inside the group to anyone outside the group. Refraining from gossip builds trust.
2. Safety: Respect each other's boundaries. Also, accept each other's perceived realities without needing to comment or "fix" how they feel or see things at the moment. Nobody should feel forced to share anything that they prefer to keep private. Providing each other space and supportive care will promote safety.
3. "I" Statements: Be yourself; take off your masks. Share information only about yourself — not "we, they, us, or you."
4. Interference: Avoid giving advice, talking while someone else is sharing, or engaging in subtle competition by saying, "I'm just like you" or by sharing a similar story. Instead, listen attentively, learn from each other's life experiences, and offer brief and affirming feedback.
5. Individuality: Accept and enjoy the diversity in your group, including being at very different places on your spiritual journeys. Allow everyone (but don't force anyone) to discover areas of need or brokenness. Avoid probing or intrusive questioning, as well as tampering with or elaborating on each other's personal sharing.
6. Emotional Sharing: Expect and allow each other to experience a full range of emotion, even if this makes you uncomfortable. This might include crying, raising a voice, or being silent. When this happens, avoid interrupting, communicating that another's feelings are unacceptable or "bad," and touching or hugging without

permission. Allow for times of quiet in your group, because silence can be one of the most powerful healing environments.
7. Roadblocks and Obstacles: It is important to allow people to process their thoughts and feelings without needing to come to clear resolution. It is also normal to experience obstacles and setbacks. Remember that being stuck can be a catalyst for members to move forward. Trust the process!
8. Holy Spirit: Only God can perform the healing and growth needed in our hearts. The purpose of the group is to provide a place where the support, love, and acceptance of God can be modeled and felt, and where the truth of God can be discovered and embraced.
9. Personal Responsibility: Recognize that true life change can only occur with God's help as we yield to His leading. The group can provide accountability through prayer and support.
10. Group Limits: Don't expect your group to provide therapy, counseling, or other in-depth one-to-one support for members. Know when to refer each other to someone outside your group who is better equipped to help.
11. Pace: Some groups study and discuss a complete chapter each week. They prepare all of the questions but only discuss selected ones. Other groups prefer to devote two weeks to each chapter. Find a pace that allows your group to truly meet with God — not just finish an academic exercise.

BENEFITS OF HEALTHY GROUP PROCESS

1. A safe place to share vulnerably and honestly.
2. New relationships.
3. An opportunity to be listened to in an accepting and grace-filled environment.
4. A forum for embracing truth, gaining perspective, and growing spiritually at your own pace.

FOR GROUP DISCUSSION: After reading these guidelines together, discuss this question among you:

Knowing myself, here are several practical things I will do to help make our group a safer place:

-
-
-

In a small group these specific things can make me feel unsafe:
-
-
-

Take time to pray as a group before you begin this journey together.

I have a Dream . . . and a Hope. I dream of a day when spiritual formation has so saturated all who follow hard after Jesus that they become known to all as experts in how to live well.

- How to love a spouse well.
- How to raise children well.
- How to study well.
- How to face adversity well.
- How to run businesses and financial institutions well.
- How to form community life well.
- How to reach out to those on the margins well.
- How to die well.

I am thinking of ordinary folk who are not known for particular customs or manner of dress or rituals, but for a particular kind of life. A life that works . . . and works well. They are of all races and classes and kinds. They are in the churches and they are outside of the churches, but they all are the Church, the people of God. Some self-identify as followers of Jesus; others, because of cultural or racial or family barriers, do not come out so publicly, but they follow hard after Jesus nonetheless. Some are followers of "the Way" without fully knowing it, for the Light of Jesus does indeed shine into the darkness and does indeed enlighten every person coming into the world (John 1:5-9). This is the saving Light of Jesus Christ, and those who turn and walk in the Light are given more Light and finally come to see that it is the Jesus Way and the Jesus Truth and the Jesus Life in which they are living.

— Richard Foster[1]

[1] *Renovaré*, October 2006, Vol. 16 No. 3, 1.

CHAPTER 1
TIME

Josh feels like he never has enough time. But he knows he wastes hours in meaningless activities. Looking back to his school days, he realizes how much more time he had then. Now the demands of his work and home just squeeze all the energy out of him. Oh, he has good intentions — to spend meaningful time with his family and with God and others. But instead, he turns instinctively to mindless entertainment when he wants to relax.

Like today. Josh's schedule is normal — stressed and mildly boring. Tomorrow looks the same. All of a sudden he stops, leans back, and asks himself, "Where in the world is my life heading? I feel like I'm on a treadmill. There's never enough time! Doesn't life have more to offer than hectic, meaningless activities? What am I missing out on?"

Can you relate to any of Josh's time struggles? Explain.

What do you do when you must decide between conflicting options for spending your time? Give an example.

As You Begin . . . Some groups decide to study and discuss a complete chapter each week. They devote about an hour individually to prepare all of the questions, but when they get together they only discuss selected questions. Other groups prefer to devote two weeks to each chapter. Find a pace that allows your group to truly meet with God — not just finish an academic exercise.

PAUSE 1_EXPLORING WHAT GOD SAYS

Time is free, but it's priceless. You can't own it, but you can use it. You can't keep it, but you can spend it. Once you've lost it, you can never get it back.

— HARVEY MACKAY

"I just don't have enough time!" We've all used that excuse, but is it really true? How about making better use of the time we have and learning the art of resting?

Our perspective on time changes with age. If we asked these people about time, what might they say?

A 25-YEAR-OLD ADULT

A 6-YEAR-OLD CHILD

AN 80-YEAR-OLD GRANDPARENT

In the column, write one insight from each verse about God's view of time.

INSIGHT ABOUT TIME

ECCLESIASTES 3:11. He has made everything beautiful in its time. He has also set eternity in the hearts of men; yet they cannot fathom what God has done from beginning to end.

MARK 6:31. Then, because so many people were coming and going that they did not even have a chance to eat, he said to them, "Come with me by yourselves to a quiet place and get some rest."

JAMES 4:14. Why, you do not even know what will happen tomorrow. What is your life? You are a mist that appears for a little while and then vanishes.

2 PETER 3:8. But do not forget this one thing, dear friends: With the Lord a day is like a thousand years, and a thousand years are like a day.

REVELATION 1:8. "I am the Alpha and the Omega — the beginning and the end," says the Lord God. "I am the one who is, who always was, and who is still to come — the Almighty One." (NLT)

From these verses, when you try to look at time from God's perspective, what do you see?

CASE STUDY: LAZARUS AND THE RICH MAN

Read the story of a rich man and a beggar named Lazarus from LUKE 16:19-31. Then respond below.

What regrets do you think the rich man might have had about the way he used his time? (verses 26-28)

Have you ever wished you could go back in time to use your time differently?

Consider these verses about the results of our choices in time.

> LUKE 16:25 (from the story you just read) and GALATIANS 6:7-9. *Do not be deceived: God cannot be mocked. A man reaps what he sows. The one who sows to please his sinful nature, from that nature will reap destruction; the one who sows to please the Spirit, from the Spirit will reap eternal life. Let us not become weary in doing good, for at the proper time we will reap a harvest if we do not give up.*

Give an example or two of times when you "reaped what you sowed" — either positively or negatively.

What if there were no consequences for people's choices in time — if we didn't reap what we sowed? How would that impact us?

LUKE 16:27-28 (from the Lazarus story) and these verses explore living life with a healthy awareness of death.

> PSALM 39:4. *Show me, O LORD, my life's end and the number of my days; let me know how fleeting is my life.*

ECCLESIASTES 7:2. It is better to go to a house of mourning than to go to a house of feasting, for death is the destiny of every man; the living should take this to heart.

ECCLESIASTES 7:4. A wise person thinks a lot about death, while a fool thinks only about having a good time. (NLT)

Has anyone close to you ever died? What is your emotional response to the thought of death and dying?

Moses essentially said, "Unless we are gripped by life's brevity and place proper value on the time we have, no matter how long or short it is, we will never gain a wise heart."

— DR. SID BUZZELL, GENERAL EDITOR, *THE LEADERSHIP BIBLE*

IDEA (FOR BRINGING PERSPECTIVE)

Talk with an elderly person on his/her perspective of time—and how it has changed over the years. Also ask how they would use their time differently if they could live their lives again.

Notes:

PAUSE 2_EXPLORING YOUR REALITY

We can employ the skills and principles of time management, buy a new calendar (even a high-priced electronic one), employ a better scheduling system — all are of little benefit until we understand the value of time. Granted, we may do a better job of scheduling our time, but that doesn't mean we're doing a better job of spending that time. Knowing the difference defines wisdom.

— DR. SID BUZZELL, GENERAL EDITOR, THE LEADERSHIP BIBLE

What is one difference between *scheduling* our time well and *spending* our time well? (See quote by Sid Buzzell.)

How would you describe the way your family used time when you were growing up? (For example, driven or laid back, on time or always late.)

VALUES AND PRIORITIES

Our time priorities can change depending on our values, our circumstances, and our seasons in life. What values drive your use of time now? From this list, <u>circle three of your top values</u> in your current season of life. Then on the chart below explain <u>how those values influence your use of time.</u>

Freedom	Efficiency	Relationships with people
Feeling meaningful or safe	Health and fitness	Intellect
Power and influence	My own space and possessions	Beauty
Intimacy with God	Other	Nature
Financial security	Fun	My image before people

VALUE...	SO I USE MY TIME TO...
Efficiency	Get my work done without spending any more time or energy than I have to

> **REALITY CHECK**
>
> *Sometimes your values conflict with each other. For example, you want to get ahead financially, but that may conflict with wanting to spend quality time with your friends or family. That happened to Jesus. In Mark 6:30-31 the crowds were hungry for teaching and hungry for food, but the disciples needed rest.*

When you "have time on your hands," what do you typically do? (For example, video gaming, sleeping, getting lost in media, etc.)

Sometimes we stay busy in order to avoid dealing with something — a problem relationship, uncomfortable feelings, fear of being alone or known, etc. Remember a time when you were busy, crazy, hectic, and running. Looking back, do you think you may have been running or hiding from something by staying busy? If so, what?

UJING YOUR JPARE TIME

Whatever hours are left over after you sleep, eat, get to and from work or school, and actually work or care for kids at home — that is your "discretionary" or your spare time. About how many hours a week of spare time do you have to do all the others things you want and need to do?

Some of us treat sleep like it's optional. Describe the typical amount and quality of your sleep and how you think it affects your waking hours.

Sleep [also is] a good reminder that we are mere creatures, not the Creator. . . . To sleep, long and soundly, is to place our trust not in our own strength and hard work, but in him without whom we labor in vain.

— LAUREN WINNER, "SLEEP THERAPY,"
HTTP://WWW.CHRISTIANVISIONPROJECT.COM/2006/01/SLEEP_THERAPY.HTML

To help you get a realistic view of how you use your spare time, consider this list. Take a guess at approximately how many hours (or minutes) you spend on these activities in a typical week.

____ Time for self
____ Time with spouse
____ Time dating
____ Time to rest
____ Time on Internet and e-mail
____ Time to do nothing
____ Other use of time (explain)
____ Time in active play
____ Time for TV, computer games, and entertainment
____ Time in community service

____ Time with children
____ Time with relatives
____ Time with friends
____ Time with God (prayer, Bible study, worship)
____ Time for personal growth, learning, and reading
____ Time for hobbies
____ Time in nature
____ Time in exercise and care of your body
____ Time just to think, reflect

Notice the top three ways you use your spare time. How well do these uses of your time reflect what you said your values are? Explain.

Sometimes we complain that we don't have enough time, but we may really mean that we don't have enough energy for everything we want to do. What might be some limitations in this season of life that you need to just accept? (See Digging Deeper for more on life's seasons.)

If you're married, consider having a conversation with your spouse about how the ways you both use your time are affecting each other and your family.

PRAYER PAUSE

Pause for a while to talk with God about how you use your time. Notice what you're experiencing emotionally and what may be distracting you as you think about your daily time choices. Talk with Him about those things, too. Thank Him for His precious gift of time. Journal any decisions He leads you to make.

PAUSE 3_
COMING ALIVE TO GOD AND OTHERS

> Moses knew time was valuable and prayed to be taught to measure it by days, not by years (Psalm 90:12). If we are careful about days, the years will care for themselves.
>
> — J. OSWALD SANDERS, SPIRITUAL LEADERSHIP

WISE USE OF TIME

Lots of voices out there try to tell us how to use our time. From these verses mark any advice about the wise use of time.

EPHESIANS 5:15-16. Be very careful, then, how you live — not as unwise but as wise, making the most of every opportunity, because the days are evil.

EPHESIANS 5:11-17. Don't waste your time on useless work, mere busywork, the barren pursuits of darkness. Expose these things for the sham they are. It's a scandal when people waste their lives on things they must do in the darkness where no one will see. Rip the cover off those frauds and see how attractive they look in the light of Christ.

Wake up from your sleep, climb out of your coffins; Christ will show you the light!

So watch your step. Use your head. Make the most of every chance you get. These are desperate times!

[17] Don't live carelessly, unthinkingly. Make sure you understand what the Master wants. (MSG)

What do you notice about a connection between wisdom and making the most of our time?

> *One thing we can't recycle is wasted time.*
> — UNKNOWN

Why do you think it's a "scandal" to "waste" our time or a season of life? (Ephesians 5:12)

What are some ways you tend to waste time or spend it "carelessly, unthinkingly"? What positive actions can you take to make wiser use of your time?

REALITY CHECK

Just as each year has different seasons, so our lives also have "seasons" that are distinct from the others. In the Digging Deeper section at the end of this chapter, you can explore how our time priorities change in different seasons of life.

RESTING

I was afraid of rest because I knew it meant embracing silence. I feared that silence would expose my heart and introduce me to a terrifying loneliness.

— SALLY BREEDLOVE, *CHOOSING REST*

God views resting as a wise use of time — both His and ours!

> GENESIS 2:3. *And God blessed (spoke good of) the seventh day, set it apart as His own, and hallowed it, because on it God rested from all His work which He had created and done.* (AMP)

Is resting easy or difficult for you in your current season of life? Explain.

How do you "honor the Sabbath" — or do you pretty much ignore it? What if you actually set aside some time each week to "savor and celebrate" God and His works and to reflect on the other six days? How might this use of your time influence your sense of satisfaction?

HISTORICAL BACKGROUND

The Hebrew word for "rested" is *shabath*. It didn't mean that God took a nap on the seventh day because He was tired. Rather, He set aside time to enjoy and savor and celebrate what He had created on the previous six days. That's what He had in mind for us to do with our Sabbath (from the same Hebrew word).

Read PSALM 23:2 and MATTHEW 11:28-29. What might it look like for you to "rest well"? How do you — or could you — get some "rest for your soul"?

PRAYER PAUSE

Jesus' words in Matthew 11 tell us that inner rest is a direct result of coming to Him. Take some unhurried time to consider anything that might prevent you from coming to Him in that way. Listen for what He might say about how rest restores your soul. We may experience serious losses of time — even a whole season of our lives — due to our own poor choices, the choices or influence of others, or just the responsibilities of life. If that has happened to you, take time to mourn those losses. You can't go back in time, but you can ask God to "repay you for the years the locusts have eaten" (Joel 2:25) in some way. Maybe He will give you a picture of how He wants to turn your loss into gain in the bigger things He's doing in you.

POINT TO PONDER

Remember that "there is a season" for everything. And a season usually lasts more than a week or two! In some life seasons, you may work fifty-plus hours a week . . . and in another season only twenty hours. Some seasons will allow for good sleep and rest. In other seasons you will be sleep deprived and you'll be grateful for a twenty-minute nap. So cut yourself some slack. You can't have everything you want at the same time, and you can't have everything you want right now or keep it perfectly balanced all the time. But you can still live well through all seasons of life.

PAUSE 4_JOURNEYING FORWARD

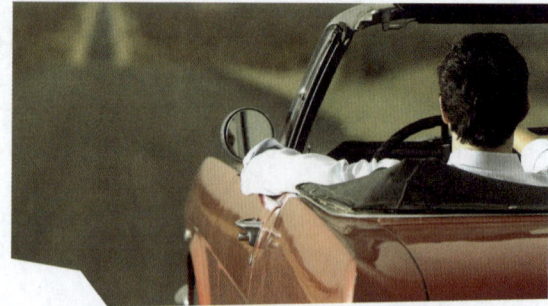

It's your life... it's your journey. So that means it's up to you how you respond to the ideas in this chapter. Pause 4 in every chapter will be like this one — completely open-ended to invite you to zero in on whatever specifically touched you most. Or whatever disturbed you the most. Whatever that is, grab on to it — don't gloss over it. During this final Pause, revisit that verse and respond to one or more of the reflective questions. Then pray about what step you should take to "walk as Jesus did" in the coming week.

How have you experienced God this week?

We live in a world of images that deeply influence how we look at life. Choose a picture from this chapter that is meaningful or disturbing to you, and briefly explain why.

At the end of each chapter we'll invite you to select one verse or passage that you read, studied, listened to, or memorized during the week that was meaningful to you. Begin by copying the verse and its reference below, so you'll be able to find it later.

Then, you'll be invited to select one or more of these reflective questions and journal your response. The point is not to answer all of the questions, but to help focus your reflection on what God is saying to you. Most chapters have a final Journal page to give you space to write.

Reflecting on what was most meaningful to you from this chapter, respond to one (or more) of these questions in the Journal on the next page:

- Who are you, Lord? (an insight into God's character or heart)
- What shall I do, Lord? (an idea for practical application)
- Who shall I be, Lord? (a sense of personal identity)
- Other response?

JOURNAL

Think of the Journal page as part of your spiritual fitness routine. Your spirit, heart, and mind have just finished some vigorous exercise. This is the cool-down phase. Not to be hurried. We suggest two things:

1. Journal on any of the preceding reflective questions.
2. Memorize and meditate on the Scripture memory verse below.

If at all possible, don't leave your study time without capturing in writing the most important things God revealed to you.

SUGGESTED MEMORY VERSE:

Every Pause 4 provides a key verse on the topic for you to memorize. See pages 185–186 for motivation and practical help on Scripture memory. You will not regret the extra effort it takes to learn these key verses by heart. Decide as a group if you will make Scripture memory part of your time together or not.

TIME — EPHESIANS 5:15-16

Be very careful, then, how you live — not as unwise but as wise, making the most of every opportunity, because the days are evil.

DIGGING DEEPER

Most chapters will include a Digging Deeper section at the end of the chapter. This is an optional exercise if you want to do some further study.

SEASONS

Just as each year has different seasons, so our lives also have "seasons" that are distinct from the others. And each season brings different time priorities.

> ECCLESIASTES 3:1. There is a time for everything, and a season for every activity under heaven.

What "season" of life are you in right now (getting more education, establishing marriage, entering career, learning to be a parent)? What might be God's primary purpose for you in your current season?

No matter which season we're in, God gives each of us the present moment as a gift. How are you experiencing (or not experiencing) God's presence now?

Have you ever sensed that God brought you to a particular moment in time that was the "right" time or season for something significant to happen to you? If so, explain.

CHAPTER 2
MONEY

Brandon barely scraped by making minimum wage at the campus coffee shop. So after graduation he was delighted when he landed an assistant manager's job. He was sure he'd pay off his credit card debt and be rolling in the dough.

Then he and Suni got married, and was it ever sweet to have two incomes pouring into the bank account. Marriage certainly had its benefits. But he never dreamed how many "extra" expenses came along with buying a house.

A promotion at work really helped . . . for a while. But then Suni got pregnant. Brandon found himself worrying about money more and more. Then their friend was going overseas to help underprivileged kids in a mission. They wanted to support him financially, but couldn't afford to. It seemed like every time they got a little more money, it was never enough. They thought they'd start out living like their parents did, but now they just couldn't figure out how to get there.

Can you relate to any part of this story? If so, how?

PAUSE 1_EXPLORING WHAT GOD SAYS

Money, houses, cars, computers, clothes, jewelry, investments, gadgets. It's the American way. Consumerism tells us that we "need" more of them to improve our status or to just keep up with everybody else. Advertisements shout, "Buy the car, get the girl! Buy the clothes, gain popularity!" It seems reasonable—even essential—to pursue financial security and buy more things. But what hidden price do we pay for our relentless drive for money? Money can wreck long-standing relationships. For instance, financial pressure is one of the leading causes of divorce. Or just watch family members fight over an inheritance. Our view of money also impacts our relationship with God. When we pursue the "almighty dollar" more than the Almighty God, we've crossed the line into the idolatry of greed. So whether you have a lot of money and things or only a little, it's important to develop healthy attitudes toward material wealth.

In His Sermon on the Mount, Jesus had a lot to say about attitudes toward money. As you read Matthew 6:19-34, jot down anything you observe about:

DANGERS OF BEING ANXIOUS OR GREEDY FOR MONEY	REASONS NOT TO WORRY ABOUT MATERIAL THINGS
verse 19—It can get stolen or wiped out at any time	verse 20—"real" treasure is always safe and never loses value

If you had a fire, what would you rush to save? Does this reveal anything about what you treasure? (verses 20-21)

Why do you think we can't serve both God and money? (verse 24)

What (if anything) do you worry about most when it comes to money or things? (verse 25)

An important promise about wealth is found in verse 33. Using "I" and "me" instead of "you" and "your," rewrite this promise in your own words.

To help put our worries into perspective, let's get real about what we already do have — especially compared to people in the rest of the world. Did you know that . . .

- . . . half the world — nearly three billion people — live on less than two dollars a day?
- . . . 30,000 children die each day due to poverty?
- . . . one out of four people on Earth don't have water in their homes, and must walk almost a mile to collect it?
- . . . Americans spend more annually on cosmetics ($8 billion) than it would cost additionally to provide basic education for all the children in developing countries ($6 billion)?
- . . . Europeans spend more annually on ice cream ($11 billion) than it would cost additionally to provide water and sanitation to all developing countries ($9 billion)?

    Source: http://www.globalissues.org/TradeRelated/Facts.asp

In light of these facts, what are you grateful for?

Instead of being anxious about what we have or don't have, we are called to be content with our money and possessions. From each of these passages, highlight and write in the margin any <u>dangers we face if we are habitually discontent</u>. Also underline any <u>reasons why we can and should be content</u>.

> 1 TIMOTHY 6:6-10. But godliness with contentment is great gain. For we brought nothing into the world, and we can take nothing out of it. But if we have food and clothing, we will be content with that. People who want to get rich fall into temptation and a trap and into many foolish and harmful desires that plunge men into ruin and destruction. For the love of money is a root of all kinds of evil. Some people, eager for money, have wandered from the faith and pierced themselves with many griefs.

> HEBREWS 13:5. Keep your lives free from the love of money and be content with what you have, because God has said, "Never will I leave you; never will I forsake you."

> JAMES 4:1-3. What causes fights and quarrels among you? Don't they come from your desires that battle within you? You want something but don't get it. You kill and covet, but you cannot have what you want. You quarrel and fight. You do not have, because you do not ask God. When you ask, you do not receive, because you ask with wrong motives, that you may spend what you get on your pleasures.

As you read these verses, did the Holy Spirit identify any unhealthy attitudes that are keeping you from being content? Explain.

What is one practical thing you can do to practice contentment? For example, whenever you purchase something new (a CD, an item of clothing, a book, a gadget, etc.), get rid of an old one.

Contentment is wanting what we have, not having what we want.
— KENTON BESHORE JR., SENIOR PASTOR, MARINER'S CHURCH, IRVINE, CALIFORNIA

It's easy for us to fall into a mindset of viewing "our" world as "the" world, because it's all we generally see. We're constantly bombarded with images of the latest styles and models of everything, and it can easily leave us feeling like what we have isn't enough because we see people that have even more than us. But how does what we have compare to what most people in the world have? Maybe what we have is enough; maybe it's more than enough. Maybe God has blessed us with everything we have so we can bless and give to others.

— HTTP://WWW.NOOMA.COM

GRATITUDE PAUSE

This would be a great time for a gratitude pause. Just stop for a few minutes and begin listing anything and everything that you are grateful for — from things to privileges to people to opportunities to basic necessities of life. Let your gratitude overflow into praise and thanks to your Father.

PAUSE 2_EXPLORING YOUR REALITY

What positive financial values or habits did you learn from your parents? Any negative ones?

THE IDOL OF MATERIALISM

Some of us have looked into the face of our idols and found that one of them is money. Though we, along with millions of other churchgoers, are saying that Jesus saves, we ask ourselves if we are not in practice acting as though it were money that saves. We say that money gives power, money corrupts, money talks. Like the ancients with their molten calf we have endowed money with our own psychic energy, giving it arms and legs, and have told ourselves that it can work for us. More than this we enshrine it in a secret place, give it a heart and a mind and the power to grant us peace and mercy.

— ELIZABETH O'CONNOR, LETTERS TO SCATTERED PILGRIMS

COLOSSIANS 3:5 says, "Don't be greedy, for a greedy person is an idolater, worshiping the things of this world" (NLT). Idolatry can be defined as anything that we trust in or turn to more than God.

Why do you think greed is a form of idolatry?

Do you ever feel "possessed by your possessions"? Examine your heart. Has greed found a home there? Explain.

The average American watches about one million commercials by age twenty (from "Americans and Money," *The Gazette*, 2006). Many advertisers try to convince us to buy their products so we'll have a desired identity.[1] Give an example of a time when some marketing or ad has:

- created a "need" in you for something you never thought you needed before
- made you feel embarrassed or ashamed that you didn't have something

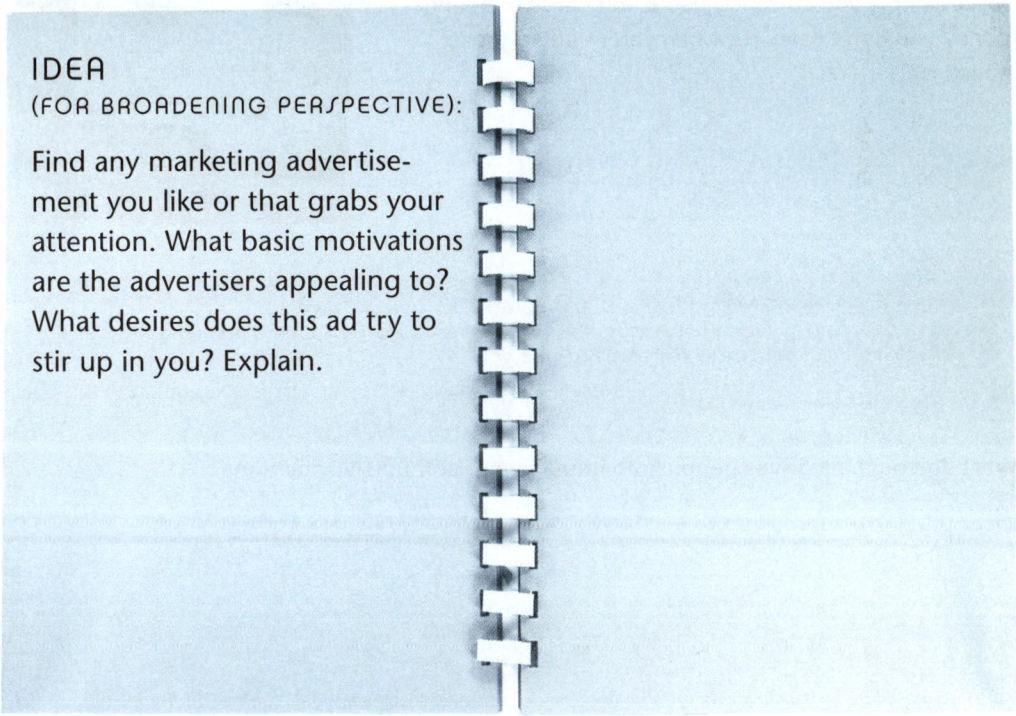

IDEA
(FOR BROADENING PERSPECTIVE):

Find any marketing advertisement you like or that grabs your attention. What basic motivations are the advertisers appealing to? What desires does this ad try to stir up in you? Explain.

CONTROLLING IMPULSIVE SPENDING

Just spending money may not be the problem. It's when we spend more money than we actually have and go into debt that we can get into trouble. It's easy to think, "Hey, everyone else is getting one; I want one, too. So why not get it now?" So we put it on our credit card or borrow money from others.

---

[1] To explore the topic of identity in more depth, see *IDENTITY: Becoming Who God Says I Am* of the CONNECT series.

An attitude of entitlement says, "I deserve to have good things — and I deserve to have them now!" Delayed gratification says, "I can wait for good things until the time is right." Describe a time when you experienced entitlement and a time when you delayed gratification.

Describe how you currently use credit cards or spend money you don't have. How can you relate to these statistics?

- *College students owe nearly half of the nation's $285 billion credit card debt.*
- *75% of U.S. adults have credit card debts of $9,000 or more. At 18% interest, and paying just the minimum balance monthly, it will take 56 years to pay off this debt.*

— "AMERICANS AND MONEY," THE GAZETTE, COLORADO SPRINGS, 2006

What do you think drives people into impulsive or compulsive spending?

TYPES OF DEBT

$ *Investment debt: usually grows in value or pays for itself over time (schooling, tools of our trade)*
$ *Pleasure debt: mostly about short-term pleasure, loses value over time (electronics, clothes)*

Practical guidelines: avoid pleasure debt, examine the risks of investment debts, and always pray before borrowing!

$ $ *Purchasing a house is also an investment debt because a house usually appreciates in value. As long as you can meet the mortgage payments every month, that's good. But consider it an investment that still has risks.*

How much and what kind of debt do you have (if any)?

How does going into debt impact you emotionally? Relationally?

Consider these seven practical options for resisting the impulse to spend unwisely. Check one or two that you would seriously consider doing in the next six months.

1. Walk away from the item immediately.
2. Compare the price of the item in three other places before you buy.
3. Buy only what is needed and practical.
4. Make a budget with spending priorities, and share these with someone who can help you stick to it.
5. Use cash, or at least limit your use of credit cards to what you can and will pay off that month.
6. Call 1-888-567-8688 to stop receiving pre-approved credit card offers in the mail.
7. Write to the following address to have your name and address removed from direct marketers' mailing lists and stop receiving lots of junk mail:

DMA Headquarters
1120 Avenue of the Americas
New York, NY 10036-6700
Fax: 212-302-6714

SAVING

As you plan ahead and think about saving money, do you usually (check any that apply):

____ Have a disciplined plan for saving money
____ Save money for a short time until you find something you really want
____ Think that you will begin to save when you are older
____ Believe that supporting a worthwhile cause is more important than saving money
____ Rely on other's savings when you are in a crisis
____ Trust that God will provide for you later, so you don't have to save now

CHALLENGE: Two college roommates decide to begin saving for their later years. One saves $2,000 a year for only six years. The other saves $2,000 a year for 31 years. At retirement, they both end up with the same amount. How can that be? And which one would you want to be? See the Digging Deeper section to find out.

What might God be saying to you about spending, debt, and savings?

PAUSE 3_COMING ALIVE TO GOD AND OTHERS

MANAGING MONEY

There are lots of places you can go for money management tips. The Bible is full of practical advice for managing our money well. It also warns us about what happens when we mismanage money. In these passages, try to find examples of each, and jot them down in the columns.

	MANAGING MONEY WELL	MISMANAGING MONEY
LUKE 3:11-15. John answered, "The man with two tunics should share with him who has none, and the one who has food should do the same." Tax collectors also came to be baptized. "Teacher," they asked, "what should we do?" "Don't collect any more than you are required to," he told them. Then some soldiers asked him, "And what should we do?" He replied, "Don't extort money and don't accuse people falsely—be content with your pay."		Cheating people out of their money
1 TIMOTHY 5:8. If anyone does not provide for his relatives, and especially for his immediate family, he has denied the faith and is worse than an unbeliever.	Be content with my pay	
JAMES 5:3-6. You [rich people] have hoarded wealth in the last days. Look! The wages you failed to pay the workmen who mowed your fields are crying out against you. The cries of the harvesters have reached the ears of the Lord Almighty. You have lived on earth in luxury and self-indulgence. You have fattened yourselves in the day of slaughter. You have condemned and murdered innocent men, who were not opposing you.		
1 TIMOTHY 6:17-19. Command those who are rich in this present world not to be arrogant nor to put their hope in wealth, which is so uncertain, but to put their hope in God, who richly provides us with everything for our enjoyment. Command them to do good, to be rich in good deeds, and to be generous and willing to share. In this way they will lay up treasure for themselves as a firm foundation for the coming age, so that they may take hold of the life that is truly life.		

What is one principle from these verses that speaks to you about the way you are handling money now? Explain.

> People must learn to handle the smallest things God has placed under their authority — their money — before He can trust them with greater things.
> — CALEB MCAFEE, MONEY AND THE CHRISTIAN

In what ways might you be tempted to put your hope in wealth? (1 Timothy 6:17)

Read LUKE 16:10-12. Think of a time when you were trusted with responsibility or someone else's money or property. How did you handle that trust? What did you learn from that experience?

GIVING

Giving to God, to church and missions, and to people in need is a beautiful act of worship. And giving helps us curb our greed and overspending. Circle the word or phrase in each pair to the right that honestly describes your usual giving attitudes and practice.

Jesus said it is more blessed to give than to receive (Acts 20:35). Describe a time when you experienced the blessing of giving.

Regular **or** Sporadic

Generous **or** Stingy

Leftovers **or** Upfront

Secretly **or** Publicly

Cheerfully **or** Out of Obligation

Freely **or** Reluctantly

No Strings Attached **or** Selfishly

Read the story of a poor widow whose giving won praise from Jesus in Luke 21:1-4. What was it about her giving that was so noteworthy? What do you think it cost this woman to give the way she did?

How does it make you feel to know that Jesus watches what we give?

Have you ever made a choice to give "out of your poverty"? What were the results?

Are there any ministries, people, or needs that God has led you to support financially? Explain.

If you could help the needy in ways other than giving money, what would you give or do?

When we choose to give, what happens as a result? Mark any promises you observe in this passage, as well as any results of your giving.

2 CORINTHIANS 9:6-15. Remember this: Whoever sows sparingly will also reap sparingly, and whoever sows generously will also reap generously. Each man should give what he has decided in his heart to give, not reluctantly or under compulsion, for God loves a cheerful giver. And God is able to make all grace abound to you, so that in all things at all times, having all that you need, you will abound in every good work. As it is written: "He has scattered abroad his gifts to the poor; his righteousness endures forever." Now he who supplies seed to the sower and bread for food will also supply and increase your store of seed and will enlarge the harvest of your righteousness. You will be made rich in every way so that you can be generous on every occasion, and through us your generosity will result in thanksgiving to God.

¹² This service that you perform is not only supplying the needs of God's people but is also overflowing in many expressions of thanks to God. Because of the service by which you have proved yourselves, men will praise God for the obedience that accompanies your confession of the gospel of Christ, and for your generosity in sharing with them and with everyone else. And in their prayers for you their hearts will go out to you, because of the surpassing grace God has given you. Thanks be to God for his indescribable gift!

What might be your next step of giving as an act of worship?

PRAYER PAUSE

Spend time alone with God. Pray over your finances and possessions. Ask God to guide your heart to surrender your money and everything you own to Him. Ask Him for guidance in the practical management of your wealth.

PAUSE 4_JOURNEYING FORWARD

PSALM 94:12. How blessed the man you train, GOD, the woman you instruct in your Word. (MSG)

PSALM 90:12. Oh! Teach us to live well! Teach us to live wisely and well! (MSG)

How have you experienced God this week?

We live in a world of images that deeply influence how we look at life. Choose a picture from this chapter that is meaningful or disturbing to you, and briefly explain why.

Select one verse or insight from this chapter that was meaningful to you this week and write it here.

From your study, respond to one of these questions in the Journal on the following page:
- Through this chapter, what has God shown you about yourself or about Him?
- What has God been saying to you about living life well in managing your money?
- What specific step of action may God want you to take in response to your study?

JOURNAL

SUGGESTED MEMORY VERSE:

MONEY — 1 TIMOTHY 6:17

Command those who are rich in this present world not to be arrogant nor to put their hope in wealth, which is so uncertain, but to put their hope in God, who richly provides us with everything for our enjoyment.

DIGGING DEEPER: THE DEBT TRAP

OVERSPENDING

Here's what overspending your income by just $80 a month will add to your debt total in five years at 18 percent annual interest, compounded annually (typical if you put that $80 on your credit card).

YEAR	DEBT ADDITION	INTEREST	TOTAL DEBT
1	$960	$173	$1,133
2	960	377	2,470
3	960	617	4,047
4	960	901	5,908
5	960	1,236	8,104

DEBT REPAYMENT

And here is what it will cost you to eliminate that debt in the next five years by repaying $216 each month, with interest compounded annually.

YEAR	REPAID ANNUALLY	INTEREST	TOTAL DEBT
6	$2,592	$1,459	$6,971
7	2,592	1,255	5,634
8	2,592	1,014	4,056
9	2,592	730	2,194
10	2,592	395	-3

Interest First 5 Years	$3,304
Interest Last 5 Years	$4,853
TOTAL Interest	$8,157
Average Annual Interest	$815
TOTAL you over-charged to Credit Card	$4,800
TOTAL you must pay back	$12,957

What do you think is the point of this illustration?

CASE STUDY: THE MAGIC OF COMPOUND INTEREST

Two college roommates decide to begin saving for their later years. Craig starts at age twenty-two and saves $166 a month. That's $2,000 a year. He puts it in an IRA each year for six years where it earns 12 percent interest annually. He leaves it in the IRA until retirement. Jason decides to get a new car before he starts saving. He's twenty-seven before he starts saving $2,000 a year in an IRA. But he has to keep saving for thirty-one years — not just six years like Craig. At retirement, they both end up with almost the same amount. How can that be?

	CRAIG				JASON		
Age	Savings		Total at End of Year	Age	Savings		Total at End of Year
22	$2000		$2,240	22	$0		$0
23	2000	**6 years**	4,749	23	0	**Bought**	0
24	2000	**of IRAs**	7,559	24	0	**a car**	0
25	2000		10,706	25	0		0
26	2000		14,230	26	0		0
27	2000		18,278	27	0		0
28	0	**Stopped**	20,359	28	2000	**Started**	2,240
29	0	**saving**	22,803	29	2000	**saving**	4,749
30	0	**for next**	25,539	30	2000	**$2,000**	7,559
31	0	**35 years**	28,603	30	2000	**every**	10,706
32	0		32,036	31	2000	**year for 35 years**	14,230
•	•	•	•	•	•		•
•	•	•	•	•	•		•
↓	↓	↓	↓	↓	↓	↓	↓
60	0		765,141	60	2000		767,042
61	0		856,958	61	2000		861,327
62	0		959,793	62	2000		966,926
63	0		1,074,968	63	2000		1,085,197
64	0		1,203,964	64	2000		1,217,661
65	0		1,348,440	65	2000		1,363,780

What do you think is the point of this story — or what principles does it reveal?

What do you think Craig gained by delaying some purchases for a few years early in life?

CHAPTER 3
BEAUTY AND PLEASURE

Bree grew up on stage. She loved the freedom that drama gave her to be anyone she wanted to be. Then at age fifteen, after her first sexual encounter, she got caught in a world of beauty that was becoming increasingly ugly to her soul. She found something powerful in her ability to tease men with her beauty. Flirting was one thing — the point was to attract. But teasing was meant to arouse. Bree had mastered both. She still enjoyed playing the game. But she also longed for more — for pleasure that wasn't so temporary, pleasure that didn't feel like it was compromising who she was.

Jason was different. His world was filled with the pleasure of his accomplishments — like designing websites at work, winning at computer games, and maintaining his nature blog. The beauty and adventure of nature really fascinated him. Beautiful women often irritated him, maybe because some seemed so shallow. But they also intimidated him, so he preferred the safety of lusting over anonymous women on the Web. When he really wanted some side pleasure, he turned to recreational drugs to get away from a nagging feeling of becoming increasingly ugly to himself and others.

How do you see Bree and Jason using their interests and desires for short-term enjoyment to avoid pain?

PAUSE 1_EXPLORING WHAT GOD SAYS

We explore the countryside for excitement, search our souls for meaning, shop the world for pleasure. We try this. Then we try that. The usual fields of endeavor are money, sex, power, adventure, and knowledge. All too often, these beautiful pleasures promise everything, but deliver nothing. Perhaps coming to grips with our futile attempts to make something with our lives will help us clear the air and get us ready for the ultimate reality — for God.

— INTRODUCTION TO ECCLESIASTES, THE MESSAGE

What kinds of beauty and pleasure are part of your everyday reality?

Enjoying beauty is part of the human experience, even if we have different ideas about what is beautiful. Maybe you're not into art, but sunsets and football games really stir your soul. Our pleasure in these things says something profound about what we were made for.

Beauty is everywhere. First, consider these verses about the beauty in nature. In the margin, identify <u>an actual place where you have experienced these kinds of beauty</u>.

> *PSALM 19:1-4. The heavens declare the glory of God; the skies proclaim the work of his hands. Day after day they pour forth speech; night after night they display knowledge. There is no speech or language where their voice is not heard. Their voice goes out into all the earth, their words to the ends of the world.*

> *ISAIAH 35:1-2. Even the wilderness and desert will rejoice in those days; the desert will blossom with flowers. Yes, there will be an abundance of flowers and singing and joy! The deserts will become as green as the Lebanon mountains, as lovely as Mount Carmel's pastures and Sharon's meadows; for the Lord will display his glory there, the excellency of our God.* (TLB)

From these verses, what does all of the beauty of nature "proclaim" and "sing" to us about?

The Song of Solomon explores another kind of beauty in depth — the beauty of human sexuality.

> SONG OF SOLOMON 1:15-17
> Young Man: "How beautiful you are, my darling, how beautiful! Your eyes are like doves."
> Young Woman: "You are so handsome, my love, pleasing beyond words! The soft grass is our bed; fragrant cedar branches are the beams of our house, and pleasant smelling firs are the rafters." (NLT)

How do you respond to knowing that God delights in sexuality and sexual beauty as He designed it to be? (NOTE: You can explore the beauty of sexuality in more depth in *SOUL: Embracing My Sexuality and Emotions* of the CONNECT series.)

After a while you notice that your life has nothing at its core. It has no center. There is activity. There is opinion. There is busyness. But there's nothing to give real pleasure or deep meaning to the activity, nothing to ground opinions in truth and shape them into convictions, nothing to translate busyness into fruitfulness, nothing to convert selfish ambition into holy purpose. . . . And you start to wonder if this is it, or were you made and called for something else?

— MARK BUCHANAN, YOUR GOD IS TOO SAFE

CASE STUDY:
SOLOMON'S SEARCH FOR MEANING IN PLEASURE AND BEAUTY

HISTORICAL BACKGROUND

When Solomon became king of Israel, he asked God for wisdom — and God made him the wisest man on earth. In his search for meaning, he also pursued all kinds of beauty and pleasure. Here's what he concluded.

ECCLESIASTES 2:1-12. I said to myself, "Let's go for it — experiment with pleasure, have a good time!" But there was nothing to it, nothing but smoke.

What do I think of the fun-filled life? Insane! Inane! My verdict on the pursuit of happiness? Who needs it? With the help of a bottle of wine and all the wisdom I could muster, I tried my level best to penetrate the absurdity of life. I wanted to get a handle on anything useful we mortals might do during the years we spend on this earth.

4-8 Oh, I did great things: built houses, planted vineyards, designed gardens and parks and planted a variety of fruit trees in them, made pools of water to irrigate the groves of trees. I bought slaves, male and female, who had children, giving me even more slaves; then I acquired large herds and flocks, larger than any before me in Jerusalem. I piled up silver and gold, loot from kings and kingdoms. I gathered a chorus of singers to entertain me with song, and — most exquisite of all pleasures — voluptuous maidens for my bed.

9-10 Oh, how I prospered! I left all my predecessors in Jerusalem far behind, left them behind in the dust. What's more, I kept a clear head through it all. Everything I wanted I took — I never said no to myself. I gave in to every impulse, held back nothing. I sucked the marrow of pleasure out of every task — my reward to myself for a hard day's work!

11 Then I took a good look at everything I'd done, looked at all the sweat and hard work. But when I looked, I saw nothing but smoke. Smoke and spitting into the wind. There was nothing to any of it. Nothing. (MSG) . . . [[but] madness and folly — NIV].

ECCLESIASTES 3:11. He has made everything beautiful in its time. He has also set eternity in the hearts of men; yet they cannot fathom what God has done from beginning to end.

What are some things that Solomon found pleasure in?

Notice that Solomon never concluded that seeking pleasure was wrong — just futile as an end in itself. Why do you think that in the midst of all this pleasure Solomon was left feeling meaningless?

Why do you think God designed us as pleasure-seeking beings in the first place? What is our thirst for beauty and pleasure meant to do for us?

GOD'S GIFT OF BEAUTY AND PLEASURE

In these verses mark anything you notice about <u>God providing pleasure and beauty for us</u>.

> PSALM 16:11. *You have made known to me the path of life; you will fill me with joy in your presence, with eternal pleasures at your right hand.*

> 1 TIMOTHY 6:17. *Command those who are rich in this present world not to be arrogant nor to put their hope in wealth, which is so uncertain, but to put their hope in God, who richly provides us with everything for our enjoyment.*

How convinced are you that God really wants you to experience enjoyment in beauty and pleasure?

Do you experience God richly providing for your enjoyment, or do you struggle with enjoying healthy pleasure or play?

PAUSE 2_EXPLORING YOUR REALITY

On the right make a list of things you take pleasure in or find beautiful. Do this quickly, without analyzing yourself.

About how much time do you spend weekly doing the things on your list?

Think of pleasure as coming in many flavors. Two of them are "recreation" and "entertainment."

- Recreation: An activity that imparts fresh life to our mind or body; something that refreshes us mentally or physically
- Entertainment: Something that amuses, pleases, or diverts our attention

Go back to the list you made. Mark each with an E (for entertainment) or R (for recreation). From your lists what do you observe about yourself?

I find pleasure (Try to list at least ten things):

Some of us have abused pleasure in the past, and that has numbed our ability to enjoy good pleasure now. Is this true of you in any way? Explain.

> *God has given us hearts wild for adventure, beauty, and intimacy. However, some of us because of wounding, training, past experiences, etc., have chosen to pursue pleasure and beauty in a "safe" way, a deadened way, a way separated from the wildness and adventure of God.*
>
> — BRENT CURTIS AND JOHN ELDREDGE, *THE SACRED ROMANCE*

What boundaries do you use to protect yourself while enjoying beauty and pleasure? What (if anything) have you seen with your eyes that you wish you hadn't seen, or what have you put into your mind that you wish you could take out? Also consider what danger you will face if you let this activity consume you.

Find an image that is ugly to you. Bring it to your group and discuss your ideas of ugliness and beauty.

Based on your study so far, are there any changes you would make in your entertainment choices?

IDEA FOR BROADENING PERSPECTIVE:

Consider giving up one form of media for a week, such as television, iPod, video games, etc. Notice what changes it makes in your life. Ask yourself:

- What experiences or feelings might our gadgets and technology be replacing or depriving us of?

- How can technology and gadgets add to our experience of beauty and pleasure?

PRAYER PAUSE

Take some time to listen to what God may be saying to you about the role of beauty and pleasure in your own life. Talk with Him about what is feeding your soul — as well as what is numbing your soul. Also ask Him if your pursuit of pleasure is connecting you closer to Him and to others — or distancing you from significant relationships. If you are finding your pleasure in things that you know are sin, consider bringing that to Him. See what He might show you or tell you.

PAUSE 3_COMING ALIVE TO GOD AND OTHERS

BEAUTY REDEEMED

Ugliness is real. We just can't be blind to the realities of our broken world and our own ugly condition apart from Christ. But God specializes in bringing good out of bad and beauty out of ugliness or brokenness. He delights in redeeming our suffering. That's what it means to participate in God's kingdom and to come alive to God and others.

Read the following Scriptures. Write on the chart anything you notice about God bringing beauty out of ugliness and restoring broken people.

> Redeem: to recover what's been lost or stolen or ruined

BROKEN	REDEEMED
Ashes	Beauty

ISAIAH 61:3. *And provide for those who grieve in Zion — to bestow on them a crown of beauty instead of ashes, the oil of gladness instead of mourning, and a garment of praise instead of a spirit of despair. They will be called oaks of righteousness, a planting of the LORD for the display of his splendor.*

EPHESIANS 5:25-27. *Husbands, love your wives, just as Christ loved the church and gave himself up for her to make her holy, cleansing her by the washing with water through the word, and to present her to himself as a radiant church, without stain or wrinkle or any other blemish, but holy and blameless.*

2 CORINTHIANS 4:16-18. *Therefore we do not lose heart. Though outwardly we are wasting away, yet inwardly we are being renewed day by day. For our light and momentary troubles are achieving for us an eternal glory that far outweighs them all. So we fix our eyes not on what is seen, but on what is unseen. For what is seen is temporary, but what is unseen is eternal.*

What else do you see from these verses about the dance between ugliness and beauty or between brokenness and wholeness?

Can pain and beauty coexist? Does anything good or meaningful ever come out of suffering? Explain.

In what ways are you engaged in creating beauty and redeeming ugliness or brokenness?

How does your experience of beauty and pleasure impact your relationship with God? Your relationships with others?

PLEASURE DEFERRED

HISTORICAL BACKGROUND
Moses would have been killed in the ethnic cleansing of his people the Israelites if the daughter of the Egyptian Pharaoh hadn't found him abandoned along the Nile River and adopted him as her son. So instead he grew up with incredible privileges, pleasures, and power. But a time came when Moses had to choose between enjoying his privilege and life of luxury as the grandson to the Pharaoh, or identifying himself with his oppressed people.

Read HEBREWS 11:24-28.

PLEASURES MOSES GAVE UP SHORT-TERM	PLEASURES MOSES GAINED LONG-TERM

Consider the example of Jesus.

> HEBREWS 12:1-3. *Therefore, since we are surrounded by such a great cloud of witnesses, let us throw off everything that hinders and the sin that so easily entangles, and let us run with perseverance the race marked out for us. Let us fix our eyes on Jesus, the author and perfecter of our faith, who for the joy set before him endured the cross, scorning its shame, and sat down at the right hand of the throne of God. Consider him who endured such opposition from sinful men, so that you will not grow weary and lose heart.*

What "ugliness" did Jesus endure for a short while for the sake of what "beauty" He would enjoy forever?

Nature and humans are incredibly beautiful. But nothing can even compare to how beautiful God is! God wants us to enjoy His beauty right in the middle of our sometimes ugly circumstances. This is how King David experienced God in the face of serious troubles.

> PSALM 96:5-6. *For all the gods of the peoples are idols, but the L*ORD *made the heavens. Splendor and majesty are before Him, strength and beauty are in His sanctuary.* (NASB)

> PSALM 27:2-4. *When evil men advance against me to devour my flesh, when my enemies and my foes attack me, they will stumble and fall. Though an army besiege me, my heart will not fear; though war break out against me, even then will I be confident. One thing I ask of the L*ORD*, this is what I seek: that I may dwell in the house of the L*ORD *all the days of my life, to gaze upon the beauty of the L*ORD *and to seek him in his temple.*

What did David find especially beautiful about God?

What do you find especially beautiful about God?

The beauty of God brings hope, comfort, and relief in the midst of life's troubles. And our thirst for beauty and pleasure draws us to God in the midst of life's troubles. Have you experienced either of these? Explain.

Is there anything hindering or entangling you now that you sense God asking you to "throw off" for the sake of living life well with Him long-term? Explain.

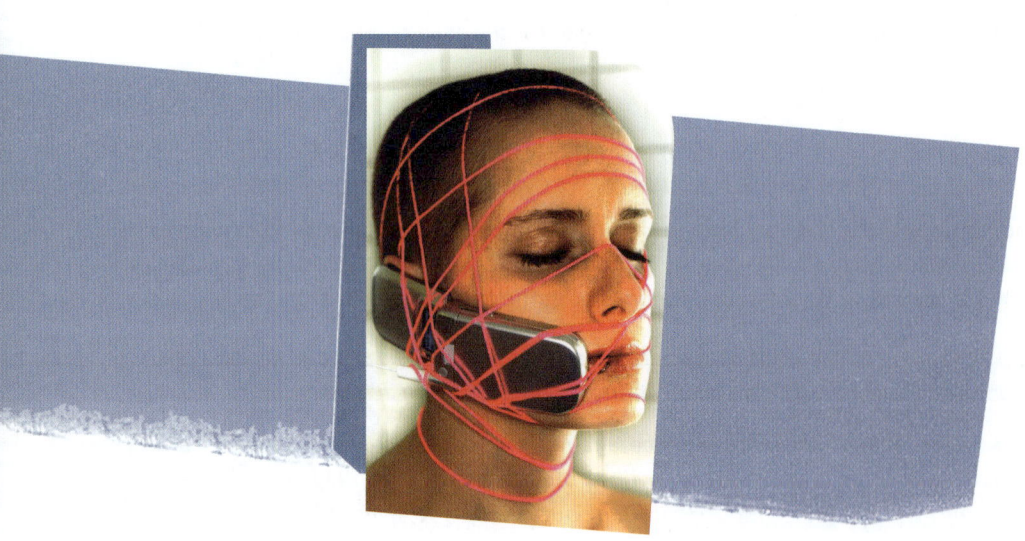

PRAYER PAUSE

Challenge yourself to take some unhurried time enjoying the incomparable beauty of God Himself, perhaps by meditating on one of these passages: 1 CHRONICLES 16:27-29; 1 CHRONICLES 29:11; and PSALM 104:1-4. See how meditating on His beauty helps connect you to your own longings, and how it exposes the cheap imitations we sometimes choose instead of real beauty.

PAUSE 4_JOURNEYING FORWARD

PSALM 94:12. How blessed the man you train, GOD, the woman you instruct in your Word. (MSG)

PSALM 90:12. Oh! Teach us to live well! Teach us to live wisely and well! (MSG)

How have you experienced God this week?

We live in a world of images that deeply influence how we look at life. Choose a picture from this chapter that is meaningful or disturbing to you, and briefly explain why.

Select one verse or insight from this chapter that was meaningful to you this week and write it here.

From your study, respond to one of these questions in the Journal on the following page:
- Through this chapter, what has God shown you about yourself or about Him?
- What has God been saying to you about beauty and pleasure?
- What specific step of action may God want you to take in response to your study?

JOURNAL

SUGGESTED MEMORY VERSE:

PLEASURE — PSALM 16:11

You have made known to me the path of life; you will fill me with joy in your presence, with eternal pleasures at your right hand.

DIGGING DEEPER

If we try to find meaning by filling our lives with pleasure, we'll be disappointed in the long run. Worse yet, we humans have a way of taking the good things God has given us and twisting them into something harmful for us or others. In these verses, highlight <u>what happens to our souls when we habitually pursue godless pleasure.</u>

> *JEREMIAH 6:10. To whom can I speak and give warning? Who will listen to me? Their ears are closed so they cannot hear. The word of the Lord is offensive to them; they find no pleasure in it.*
>
> *EPHESIANS 4:19. Having lost all sensitivity, they have given themselves over to sensuality so as to indulge in every kind of impurity, with a continual lust for more.*
>
> *2 TIMOTHY 3:4. [They will be] treacherous [betrayers], rash, [and] inflated with self-conceit. [They will be] lovers of sensual pleasures and vain amusements more than and rather than lovers of God.* (AMP)

Jot down some observations about the long-term consequences of indulging ourselves with short-term godless pleasure.

Certain kinds of beauty (especially sexual beauty) can lead to lust. How can we admire beauty without stepping over the line into lust?

How could you begin filling life with pleasure in God that pushes out the counterfeits?

CHAPTER 4
MY BODY

The health spa, the whole foods store, the cosmetic counter, the nail salon, and her favorite clothing boutique — Jillian hopes that all of these will keep her "looking good in the mirror." Lately she wonders, "Am I doing the right things for the wrong reasons?" She admits that her self-image revolves around her image in the mirror — "Do I like what I see? Do women envy what they see? Do men desire what they see?"

Jake stays fit and takes supplements but isn't particularly muscular. Recently he's been asking himself, "How can women see my inner strength if I'm not buff?"

Sarah has battled several body issues related to hormones: acne started early, her breasts developed late, and now it's facial hair. Frankly she hates her body and blames it for her social struggles. Lately she's been asking, "Why can't I just be a normal woman? Will anybody see the real me trapped inside this ugly body?"

Tim wonders, "Why do I always eat when I'm not hungry and cram my mouth with junk food?" Lots of beer and chips while watching football used to feel just fine.

What needs or voids might these people be trying to fill by focusing (or not focusing) on their bodies?

Which person's story do you connect with, and why?

PAUSE 1_EXPLORING WHAT GOD SAYS

This whole Bible study series is about our *spiritual* transformation. So why even discuss our *physical* bodies? Well, for one thing, our bodies are among God's greatest and most mysterious gifts to us, and they are a big part of our identity. It's too easy to put our bodies right at the center of our lives by obsessing over feeding, adorning, pampering, and protecting them. Before long we can be tricked into thinking that life is all about our bodies. We may even grow to hate our bodies when they betray us by being less than perfect (as defined by the trendsetters around us) or when they have the nerve to get sick or old. We may even try various high-risk behaviors and ignore the consequences. Honoring God with our bodies is an important part of our spiritual formation journey. After all, God made us as whole, integrated beings. So we can't expect the "inner person" to be truly transformed without also paying attention to the "outer person."

When God created human beings He called us "very good" (Genesis 1:31) — that included our bodies. What do you think was so "good" or beautiful about us physically in God's eyes?

Consider what the Bible says about our bodies and their basic needs.

> *MATTHEW 6:25,31-33. That is why I tell you not to worry about everyday life — whether you have enough food and drink, or enough clothes to wear. Isn't life more than food, and your body more than clothing? . . . So don't worry about these things, saying, "What will we eat? What will we drink? What will we wear?" These things dominate the thoughts of unbelievers, but your heavenly Father already knows all your needs. Seek the Kingdom of God above all else, and live righteously, and he will give you everything you need.* (NLT)

> *1 CORINTHIANS 6:19-20. Don't you realize that your body is the temple of the Holy Spirit, who lives in you and was given to you by God? You do not belong to yourself, for God bought you with a high price. So you must honor God with your body.* (NLT)

From these passages, what are a few basic truths that God wants us to understand about our bodies?

> For usual human beings in the usual circumstances, their body runs their life. Contrary to the words of Jesus in Matthew 6:25, life is, for them, not more than food, nor the body more than clothing. As a matter of simple fact, their time and energy is almost wholly, if not entirely, devoted to how their body looks, smells, and feels, and to how it can be secured and used to meet ego needs such as admiration, sexual gratification, and power over others. It is this bodily orientation of the self that runs the human cosmos.
>
> — DALLAS WILLARD, *RENOVATION OF THE HEART*

Why do you think so many people are wrapped up in their material needs like food and clothing, as though "their body runs their life" (see above Dallas Willard quote)?

From 1 Corinthians 6:19-20 (page 66), who owns your body, and who does not own your body? What difference does that make in living well?

What counsel do these next passages offer in terms of honoring God with our physical bodies?

HONORING GOD BY . . .

ROMANS 12:1-2. And so, dear brothers, I plead with you to give your bodies to God. Let them be a living sacrifice, holy — the kind he can accept. When you think of what he has done for you, is this too much to ask? Don't copy the behavior and customs of this world, but be a new and different person with a fresh newness in all you do and think. Then you will learn from your own experience how his ways will really satisfy you. (TLB)

ROMANS 6:12-13. Therefore do not let sin reign in your mortal body so that you obey its evil desires. Do not offer the parts of your body to sin, as instruments of wickedness, but rather offer yourselves to God, as those who have been brought from death to life; and offer the parts of your body to him as instruments of righteousness.

2 CORINTHIANS 7:1. Since we have these promises, dear friends, let us purify ourselves from everything that contaminates body and spirit, perfecting holiness out of reverence for God.

From these passages, list one or two primary purposes for our bodies.

Now go back over what you've written on the last two pages. Write several examples of how you can honor God with your body, such as:

> Don't copy the behavior and customs of this world. I won't go into debt to buy clothes just to be "in style."

YOUR EXAMPLES:

God is in the process of transforming all of us — including our bodies and our sexuality[1]. From this passage about the value and importance of our bodies, mark several different reasons <u>why God cares so much about our bodies</u>.

> *1 CORINTHIANS 6:12-20. You say, "I am allowed to do anything" — but not everything is good for you. And even though "I am allowed to do anything," I must not become a slave to anything. You say, "Food was made for the stomach, and the stomach for food." (This is true, though someday God will do away with both of them.) But you can't say that our bodies were made for sexual immorality. They were made for the Lord, and the Lord cares about our bodies. And God will raise us from the dead by his power, just as he raised our Lord from the dead.*
>
> *[15] Don't you realize that your bodies are actually parts of Christ? Should a man take his body, which is part of Christ, and join it to a prostitute? Never! And don't you realize that if a man joins himself to a prostitute, he becomes one body with her? For the Scriptures say, "The two are united into one." But the person who is joined to the Lord is one spirit with him.*
>
> *[18] Run from sexual sin! No other sin so clearly affects the body as this one does. For sexual immorality is a sin against your own body. Don't you realize that your body is the temple of the Holy Spirit, who lives in you and was given to you by God? You do not belong to yourself, for God bought you with a high price. So you must honor God with your body.* (NLT)

---

[1] Of course the Bible has lots more to say about this important subject — so much that most of the study *SOUL: Embracing My Sexuality and Emotions* in this series is devoted to exploring our sexual identity.

What is your emotional response to this passage?

Since God values our bodies as His temple, what do you think it means that sexual immorality is "a sin against your own body" (verse 18)?

As a mature and competent individual, I am responsible for the care of my body, and it is the center of all the other responsibilities I have. But that does not imply that I and I alone have the right to say what is to be done with it, or in short, that I own my body. . . . It is therefore God's to do with as he pleases, and he pleases that our body should be "a showplace of God's greatness" (1 Corinthians 6:20, PAR). Christians are the last people on earth who should say, "My body is my own, and I shall do with it what I please."

— DALLAS WILLARD, RENOVATION OF THE HEART

PRAYER PAUSE

Prayerfully consider this quote. Are you making any choices that essentially declare, "My body is my own, and I'll do whatever I want with it" — even if it doesn't please God? Explain.

PAUSE 2_EXPLORING YOUR REALITY

FREE ASSOCIATION:

Jot down the first two or three things that come to your mind below.

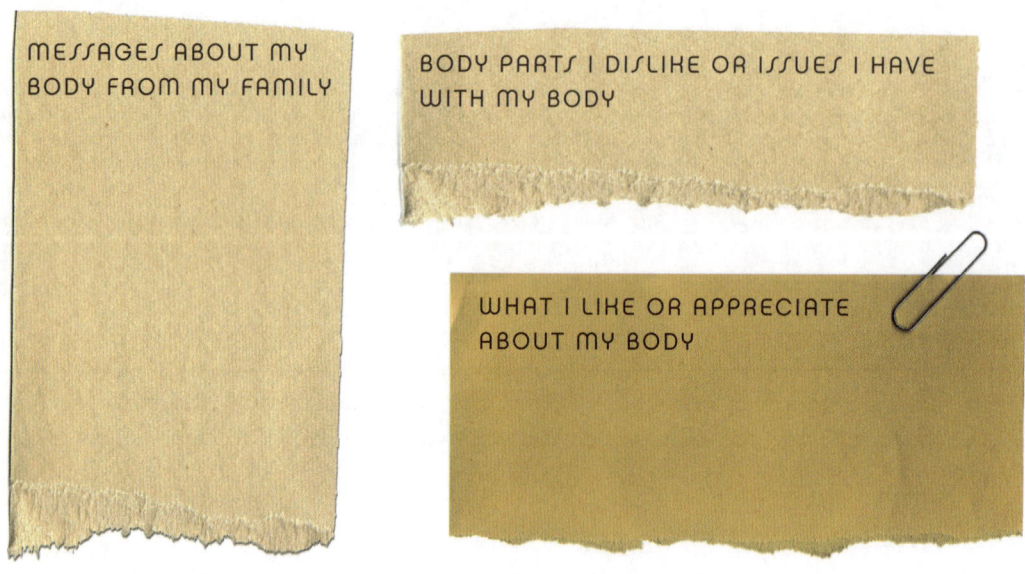

As we grow older, everyone suffers some loss of mental and physical capabilities. So will you. How do you feel about this fact? How do you act in light of this fact?

The people around us can have a huge impact on how we treat our bodies. When it comes to what we do (or don't do) with our bodies, list some ways that other people can:

- influence us negatively

- influence us positively

Think about your current patterns of eating, sleeping, and exercising. If you could make one change in one of those areas to take better care of your body, what would it be?

Consider this list of high-risk activities that can seriously damage our bodies — as well as our hearts and lives. We're not asking you to check the ones you've engaged in. Instead, think of someone you know who has engaged in one or more of these activities. How do you think they feel when they're actually doing it? What feelings or consequences do you think they might be trying to avoid by taking these risks? (If you don't know, consider talking with your friend about his/her behavior.)

- Alcohol abuse
- Drug abuse
- Smoking
- Addictions
- Asphyxiation
- Cutting/self-harm
- Food binging
- Eating disorders
- Sex outside marriage
- Reckless driving
- Extreme-risk sports
- Abortion
- Other?

Like almost anything, taking care of our bodies can be taken to extremes. Sometimes we allow our bodies to take center stage in our lives. Maybe we obsess over our bodies by indulging and pampering them or by forming compulsive addictions. On the other hand, we may neglect, abuse, or even punish our bodies. List here any behavior of yours (or others) that fit these categories:

NEGLECTING, ABUSING, OR PUNISHING YOUR BODY:	INDULGING OR OVERPAMPERING YOUR BODY:	GOOD HABITS THAT NURTURE OR PROTECT YOUR BODY:

Here are some other attitudes and behaviors that are like flashing lights on a dashboard. They may indicate (but don't always) that we've gotten dangerously out-of-balance in our view of bodies — our own or others. As you read over this list, identify any that you have struggled with significantly either now or in the past.

- Despair over normal losses (hearing, memory, hair, vigor, etc.)
- "Worship" of youth
- Racial appearance
- Excessive drive for plastic surgery
- Disappointment about our future
- Suicidal thoughts or attempts
- Shame/disgust at overweight or old people
- Immodest/sexy dressing
- Anger or fear of death and dying
- Being bullied/verbal abuse
- Sexualization of anything or everything
- Depression or anxiety
- Fear of illness or disease
- Frenzy over physical attractiveness
- Other?

Respond to one item from this list, either from personal experience or observation.

PRAYER PAUSE

Has God used this study so far to call your attention to any body issue or behavior that you need to address? Is there a habit or attitude or some aspect of your physical life that you long for God to touch, heal, or transform? Whether your list of body concerns is long and life-threatening or just the need for a routine dental check-up, pause now to talk with the Holy Spirit about any of these things. Ask Him to reveal the seriousness of your concern as well as how it has impacted your heart and spiritual journey. Ask Him what first step you could take to address whatever you're concerned about. And don't try to do it alone. Also ask Him who else you could talk to and get help from. And invite Him to help you receive His mercy and acceptance in the process.

PAUSE 3_COMING ALIVE TO GOD AND OTHERS

GOD'S GIFTS TO THE BODY

God has given lots of good gifts to our bodies — like food and sleep. Our role is to keep our bodies healthy and available to glorify Him by appreciating His good gifts within boundaries. But too much of a good thing (or not enough) can be a bad thing.

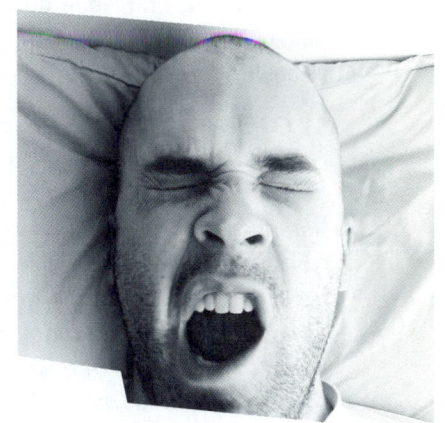

Select <u>one</u> or more of the topics below that interests you about living well with your body, and study the verses listed.

God's Gift of Sleep	God's Gift of Exercise & Movement
Proverbs 19:15 Proverbs 20:13 Proverbs 24:33-34	1 Timothy 4:8 1 Corinthians 9:24-27 Psalm 149:3
God's Gift of Drink	God's Gift of Aging
1 Timothy 5:23 Ephesians 5:18 ✖ Proverbs 23:20-21	Isaiah 46:3-4 2 Corinthians 4:16-18 2 Corinthians 5:1-5 Psalm 73:26
God's Gift of Food Proverbs 23:1-3 ▲ 1 Corinthians 8:7 1 Timothy 4:1-5	✖ *Debauchery* means "the habit of indulging ourselves in sensually or morally corrupt behaviors." ▲ *Gluttony* means "the habit of eating or drinking excessively."

Now sum up what you noticed about using God's gift of _____ well:

ACCEPTING LIMITATIONS AND DISABILITIES

Ours is not the first generation to struggle with body issues. Even the apostle Paul struggled with a significant physical limitation.

> 2 CORINTHIANS 12:7-10. *Because of the extravagance of those revelations, and so I wouldn't get a big head, I was given the gift of a handicap to keep me in constant touch with my limitations. Satan's angel did his best to get me down; what he in fact did was push me to my knees. No danger then of walking around high and mighty! At first I didn't think of it as a gift, and begged God to remove it. Three times I did that, and then he told me, "My grace is enough; it's all you need. My strength comes into its own in your weakness." Once I heard that, I was glad to let it happen. I quit focusing on the handicap and began appreciating the gift. It was a case of Christ's strength moving in on my weakness. Now I take limitations in stride, and with good cheer, these limitations that cut me down to size — abuse, accidents, opposition, bad breaks. I just let Christ take over! And so the weaker I get, the stronger I become.* (MSG)

With Paul's example in mind, how might you rely on God's grace as you struggle with a body issue or limitation?

God uses my hearing loss to crowd me to Himself. I've experienced so much spiritual transformation through my limitation.

— DEBBIE ENTSMINGER, COLLEGIATE STAFF, THE NAVIGATORS

How might God meet you (or how has He already met you) in the pain of your unresolved body issues? How might He use your body issues in your spiritual transformation process?

> PSALM 16:5-6. *L*ORD*, you have assigned me my portion and my cup; you have made my lot secure. The boundary lines have fallen for me in pleasant places; surely I have a delightful inheritance.*

Who is on your team as you seek to take care of your body?

How can you come alongside and offer support to friends with special needs, disabilities, or limitations?

> *Spiritual transformation requires the transformation of the body. The proper retraining and nurturing of the body is absolutely essential to Christ-likeness. The body is not just a physical thing. As it matures, it increasingly takes on the quality of "inner" life . . . [until] the deeds and words of Jesus become a natural expression of who we are.*
>
> — DALLAS WILLARD, *RENOVATION OF THE HEART*

CELEBRATING TRANSFORMATION

Take some time to celebrate what you do have in your body and all it does for you — rather than focusing on what you don't have or what you can't do. Let PHILIPPIANS 4:8 guide you to appreciate what is good and gracious and lovely about your physical frame and how this can reveal God.

From these verses, what will happen to our bodies when we reach heaven?

PHILIPPIANS 3:21

1 CORINTHIANS 15:42-44

Whatever body issues you may struggle with, what comfort and hope do you find in these verses about the destiny of your transformed body?

When you consider that God chooses to actually live in us (2 Corinthians 6:16), how specifically will you nurture or care for your body well? (See Digging Deeper for more ideas.)

PRAYER PAUSE

Let David's prayer below guide your conversation with God about how He has created you. Journal about whatever you hear God saying to you about you and your body.

> *PSALM 139:13-16. You made all the delicate, inner parts of my body and knit me together in my mother's womb. Thank you for making me so wonderfully complex! Your workmanship is marvelous — how well I know it. You watched me as I was being formed in utter seclusion, as I was woven together in the dark of the womb. You saw me [my unformed body — NIV] before I was born. Every day of my life was recorded in your book. Every moment was laid out before a single day had passed.* (NLT)

PAUSE 4_JOURNEYING FORWARD

*PSALM 94:12. How blessed the man you train, G*OD*, the woman you instruct in your Word.* (MSG)

PSALM 90:12. Oh! Teach us to live well! Teach us to live wisely and well! (MSG)

How have you experienced God this week?

We live in a world of images that deeply influence how we look at life. Choose a picture from this chapter that is meaningful or disturbing to you, and briefly explain why.

Select one verse or insight from this chapter that was meaningful to you this week and write it here.

From your study, respond to one of these questions in the Journal on the following page:
- Through this chapter, what has God shown you about yourself or about Him?
- What has God been saying to you about living life well in respecting your body?
- What specific step of action may God want you to take in response to your study?

JOURNAL

SUGGESTED MEMORY VERSE:

MY BODY — 1 CORINTHIANS 6:19-20

Don't you realize that your body is the temple of the Holy Spirit, who lives in you and was given to you by God? You do not belong to yourself, for God bought you with a high price. So you must honor God with your body. (NLT)

DIGGING DEEPER

God gifted us with our bodies and wants us to enjoy them. Even more astounding, He chose our bodies as His temple and dwelling place (2 Corinthians 6:16). Consider these practical ways to let God live in you.

1. **Intentionally release your body to God.** Consider a private ceremony to dedicate your body to God, perhaps on a yearly basis.

- Take an extended, unrushed time alone with God to quiet your soul and relax your body.
- Meditatively pray over some Scriptures, especially about the body.
- Slowly surrender your body to God, one part at a time.
- Ask God to take charge of your body, to fill it with His life, and to use it for His purposes.
- Get up and spend time praising God with your entire being — body, soul, spirit, emotions, and mind.

— Adapted from Dallas Willard, *Renovation of the Heart*

2. **Honor God through resting.** Take the Sabbath seriously. It is God's sacred gift to your body. When you come to the place where you can joyously "do no work," it will be because you can trust Him with your life enough to take your hands off the steering wheel.

- Take an extended, unrushed time alone with God to quiet your soul and relax your body.
- Praise God for His work throughout time.
- Praise God for His work in and through you this past week.
- Praise God for His work in and through others this past week.

Journal your experience of "presenting" your body to God.

Journal your experience of "resting."

CHAPTER 5
WORK

Colton struggles constantly at work with feeling powerless and meaningless. And he's frustrated that he can't afford to move out of his parents' house. Sometimes he blames it on not getting enough education or not knowing the right people. The bottom line is that he is tired of the work he has to do. It's the same routine every day — drudgery and boredom.

As a follower of Jesus, Colton doesn't like going to work with a resentful attitude. But he just can't seem to find a way to get what he wants. And that's another problem. He's really not sure what he wants except more money and more free time. He has dreams and passion, but he can't see how to reach for them while he's stuck in his dead-end job.

Recently he was struck by a simple thought — Jesus was a sweaty carpenter for a lot of years. Did the Son of God ever feel meaningless at His work?

Can you relate to Colton in any way?

Recommended Resources for exploring possible vocations:
IDENTITY: Becoming Who God Says I Am (CONNECT series), Chapters 7–10
BreakThru: Discovering My Spiritual Gifts
BreakThru: Discovering My Primary Roles

PAUSE 1_EXPLORING WHAT GOD SAYS

We spend most of our waking hours either preparing for or doing work. If we can find satisfaction in the work we do, it really helps our outlook on life. But if there is little meaning to our work, then life can quickly become drudgery. When we love what we do, our work can be thrilling. But realistically, much of the time it's quite thorny. In this study we'll also try to see work as something larger than just employment or what we do for a paycheck. The "work of our hands" might be a passion we pursue outside of our daily workplace. We'll start by exploring God's purposes for our work.

THE ORIGIN OF WORK

Read the following passages and look for what important responsibilities God assigned to men and women.

> GENESIS 1:26-28; 2:15. Then God said, "Let us make man in our image, in our likeness, and let them rule over the fish of the sea and the birds of the air, over the livestock, over all the earth, and over all the creatures that move along the ground." So God created man in his own image, in the image of God he created him; male and female he created them. God blessed them and said to them, "Be fruitful and increase in number; fill the earth and subdue it. Rule over the fish of the sea and the birds of the air and over every living creature that moves on the ground." . . . The LORD God took the man and put him in the Garden of Eden to work it and take care of it.

The first two commands given to humans were about their life's work:

1. The **Culture Command** ("be fruitful . . . increase in number . . . fill the earth" — Genesis 1:28) tasked us to create all the families, societies, and cultures of the world — as well as all of the systems needed to sustain them.
2. The **Nature Command** ("rule over every living creature" and "work [the Garden of Eden] and take care of it" — Genesis 2:15) tasked us with the stewardship of nature and the environment.

How do you think the Culture and Nature Commands might still apply to people today?

In what ways might the work you do (or the work you're training to do) contribute to either the Culture Command or the Nature Command or both?

Mark anything these passages reveal about why God wants us to work.

> *1 THESSALONIANS 4:11-12. Make it your ambition to lead a quiet life, to mind your own business and to work with your hands, just as we told you, so that your daily life may win the respect of outsiders and so that you will not be dependent on anybody.*
>
> *1 TIMOTHY 5:8. But those who won't care for their relatives, especially those in their own household, have denied the true faith. Such people are worse than unbelievers.* (NLT)
>
> *EPHESIANS 4:28. He who has been stealing must steal no longer, but must work, doing something useful with his own hands, that he may have something to share with those in need.*

Where are you now on your journey from dependence to independence in your work?

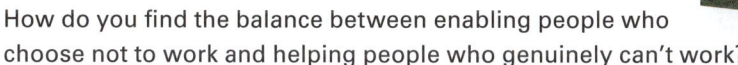

How do you find the balance between enabling people who choose not to work and helping people who genuinely can't work?

From Ephesians 2:10 explain what you think it means that:

- We are "God's workmanship."

- We are "created . . . to do good works."

How might God use you to appropriately help those who don't get income or can't work? (Ephesians 4:28)

THE SATISFACTION/THRILL OF WORK

In the Bible, the concept of work includes employment — but it includes much more. What do you think is the difference between "doing work" and "being employed"? Give some examples of each.

If the Caller is real — if there is in fact a God who calls us to places — we can reasonably expect that He knows whom He's calling. And if He knows us, it seems safe to conclude that He has insights into our talents and the world in which we use them. Isn't it likely, then, that in learning to hear and respond to His voice, we'll learn to engage with the work world — as teachers, lawyers, mothers, administrators, or some combo platter — more wisely?

— CONNALLY GILLIAM, REVELATIONS OF A SINGLE WOMAN

Compare this passage with the quote above.

> ROMANS 12:6-8. *We have different gifts, according to the grace given us. If a man's gift is prophesying, let him use it in proportion to his faith. If it is serving, let him serve; if it is teaching, let him teach; if it is encouraging, let him encourage; if it is contributing to the needs of others, let him give generously; if it is leadership, let him govern diligently; if it is showing mercy, let him do it cheerfully.*

How does God want to use our unique design in whatever work He gives us in His kingdom, as well as whatever work we find to do for employment?

When we look back on our lives, many of us will conclude that our greatest contribution to the world — our most significant "life work" — wasn't done for a paycheck at all. It might be raising kids, writing a book, planting trees, discipling and mentoring people, or fundraising for a charity. Wherever you are now in your life, what nonpaid work are you most passionate about doing? Or is that even on your radar screen? Explain.

THE THORNS OF WORK

The reality is that we don't live in the Garden of Eden. We live in a broken, fallen world. From this passage, highlight what <u>impact the Fall had on the initial thrill of the work</u> God gave us to do.

> GENESIS 3:16-19. *To the woman he said, "I will greatly increase your pains in childbearing; with pain you will give birth to children. Your desire will be for your husband, and he will rule over you."*

17 To Adam he said, "Because you listened to your wife and ate from the tree about which I commanded you, 'You must not eat of it,' Cursed is the ground because of you; through painful toil you will eat of it all the days of your life. It will produce thorns and thistles for you, and you will eat the plants of the field. By the sweat of your brow you will eat your food until you return to the ground, since from it you were taken; for dust you are and to dust you will return."

What part of your current work (both the paid and the unpaid kind) is "painful" (verse 16) or "thorny" (verse 18) to you?

What do you do with your disappointment when your expectations about your work aren't met?

Is there any good to be found in the thorns of work? How can these thorns impact your spiritual transformation? Explain.

Work can be satisfying, but it can also be frustrating. David's son Solomon did intense personal research on the topic of work satisfaction — and dissatisfaction. As you read these passages, use different colored highlighters or different markings to identify any sources of frustration and sources of satisfaction with work.

ECCLESIASTES 2:17-25. *So I hated life, because the work that is done under the sun was grievous to me. All of it is meaningless, a chasing after the wind. I hated all the things I had toiled for under the sun, because I must leave them to the one who comes after me. And who knows whether he will be a wise man or a fool? Yet he will have control over all the work into which I have poured my effort and skill under the sun. This too is meaningless. So my heart began to despair over all my toilsome labor under the sun. For a man may do his work with wisdom, knowledge and skill, and then he must leave all he owns to someone who has not worked for it. This too is meaningless and a great misfortune. What does a man get for all the toil and anxious striving with which he labors under the sun? All his days his work is pain and grief; even at night his mind does not rest. This too is meaningless. A man can do nothing better than to eat and drink and find satisfaction in his work. This too, I see, is from the hand of God, for without him, who can eat or find enjoyment?*

ECCLESIASTES 3:22. So I saw that there is nothing better for a man than to enjoy his work, because that is his lot. For who can bring him to see what will happen after him?

ECCLESIASTES 5:19. Moreover, when God gives any man wealth and possessions, and enables him to enjoy them, to accept his lot and be happy in his work — this is a gift of God.

Sum up one thing that touches you or connects with your work reality from these passages.

Does your work ever feel meaningless? Do Solomon's words give you any new perspective?

Have you ever considered enjoying your income and being happy in work as a gift from God and His Fatherly way of providing for you (Ecclesiastes 5:19)? Explain.

PRAYER PAUSE

Talk to God about the thrills and the thorns of work. What would you like to ask of God and thank God for regarding your work?

PAUSE 2_EXPLORING YOUR REALITY

When it comes to our work, an attitude of entitlement might say, "I should start out with a good salary, get perks now, be the boss, and manage my own time in my own way as long as I get my work done on time."

List anything you've ever done to earn money.

CASE STUDY

Mark graduated last year from a good college with a bachelor's degree in business. His professors used to assure the business majors that they would make fabulous salaries. A year has passed. Mark has turned down three good job offers because he is convinced that he deserves to start out with a larger salary. He can't understand why it's taking so long. He was passionate about business and he figured he should get paid to pursue his passion. Now he wonders if he was expecting too much too soon.

If Mark asked you for advice, what would you tell him?

When you were growing up, what career or work did you imagine yourself doing someday? What happened to that dream?

Does your current work or schooling feel like a blessing or a curse to you — or something in between? How do those emotions affect the way you do your job and/or schoolwork? Explain.

How have you seen God use people in ordinary jobs to advance His kingdom? Explain.

How can your current job waiting tables, crunching numbers, caring for children, or whatever, become an avenue for others to experience God's kindness and truth? (Romans 2:4)

IDEA A

Have you ever considered how you would feel if you couldn't work? Interview someone who isn't working now—someone who has been disabled or fired or forced to retire earlier than they wanted to. Find out how they feel about their lack of work. Record your findings:

IDEA B

Or do you know someone who absolutely loves his/her job? Contact that person and find out what is so appealing about the work, and why it gives such satisfaction. Record your findings:

Do you ever throw yourself into your work in order to escape the "work of relationships"? What have been the long-term outcomes of your choices?

What makes (or would make) you feel satisfied or meaningful at work?

Our society attaches value and worth to the salaries we receive. How important is it to you to receive a high income at your job, and why?

What emotions would you feel if you were permanently disabled and couldn't work? What do these emotions reveal about the importance and meaning of work to you?

PRAYER PAUSE

How might God be using your current work/school situation in the process of your spiritual transformation? Talk to God about experiencing His presence in your workplace.

PAUSE 3_
COMING ALIVE TO GOD AND OTHERS

In New Testament times, many people worked all their lives as slaves or servants in other people's households and businesses. It was a common form of employment. So in these passages try to see beyond the "slave-master" terms that offend us today. Look for any basic <u>principles of employee-employer relationships and work attitudes</u>. Summarize them in the chart on the following page.

> **BROADENING YOUR PERSPECTIVE**
>
> NOTE: Many factors contribute to a healthy work life, including managing time, handling money honestly, making ethical decisions, and respecting authority. You will study each of these topics in more depth in other chapters in this study. For now, consider how we can come alive to God and how we can treat others well in our work contexts.

EPHESIANS 6:5-7. Slaves, obey your earthly masters with deep respect and fear. Serve them sincerely as you would serve Christ. Try to please them all the time, not just when they are watching you. As slaves of Christ, do the will of God with all your heart. Work with enthusiasm, as though you were working for the Lord rather than for people. (NLT)

COLOSSIANS 3:22–4:1. Slaves, obey your earthly masters in everything; and do it, not only when their eye is on you and to win their favor, but with sincerity of heart and reverence for the Lord. Whatever you do, work at it with all your heart, as working for the Lord, not for men, since you know that you will receive an inheritance from the Lord as a reward. It is the Lord Christ you are serving. Anyone who does wrong will be repaid for his wrong, and there is no favoritism.

^{4:1} Masters, provide your slaves with what is right and fair, because you know that you also have a Master in heaven.

2 THESSALONIANS 3:10-12. For even when we were with you, we gave you this rule: "If a man will not work, he shall not eat." We hear that some among you are idle. They are not busy; they are busybodies. Such people we command and urge in the Lord Jesus Christ to settle down and earn the bread they eat.

	WORK ATTITUDES	WORK ETHICS	EMPLOYER-EMPLOYEE RELATIONSHIPS
EPHESIANS 6:5-9	Vs. 6-7 work with all my heart & enthusiastically	V. 6 work hard even when nobody is watching	V. 5 obey my boss with deep respect
COLOSSIANS 3:22–4:1			
2 THESSALONIANS 3:10-12			

How does your work help you connect with others and build community?

What special challenges do you think people face when God calls them into "ministry" as their vocation, such as a pastor or missionary?

HISTORICAL BACKGROUND

The Gospels report that Jesus worked as a carpenter, probably learning the trade from His earthly father, Joseph, until He was approximately thirty years old (Mark 6:3). Only in the last three years of His life did He devote Himself exclusively to His heavenly Father's work in the ministry of the gospel.

Do you think Jesus' work as a carpenter was insignificant or meaningless? Why, or why not? If not, what do you think the first thirty years of Jesus' life and work as a carpenter contributed to His three years in ministry?

> The sense that all of life must be lived for God opens all vocations to the possibility for spiritual influence. . . . Thus believers must permeate society. Christians need to live with integrity and make distinctive contributions in the social, scientific, artistic, educational, and political life of the nation.
>
> — DON E. EBERLY, *RESTORING THE GOOD SOCIETY*

How do you see the work you are doing now (or the work you are training to do):

- opening up possibilities for spiritual influence?

- glorifying God?

What barriers (if any) do you face supporting yourself, supporting your family/household, and contributing to those in need?

What practical step can you take in the next six to twelve months to move toward responsible financial independence? Or who can help you?

PAUSE 4_JOURNEYING FORWARD

PSALM 94:12. How blessed the man you train, GOD, the woman you instruct in your Word. (MSG)

PSALM 90:12. Oh! Teach us to live well! Teach us to live wisely and well! (MSG)

How have you experienced God this week?

We live in a world of images that deeply influence how we look at life. Choose a picture from this chapter that is meaningful or disturbing to you, and briefly explain why.

Select one verse or insight from this chapter that was meaningful to you this week and write it here.

From your study, respond to one of these questions in the Journal on the following page:

- Through this chapter, what has God shown you about yourself or about Him?
- What has God been saying to you about living life well in work?
- What specific step of action may God want you to take in response to your study?

JOURNAL

SUGGESTED MEMORY VERSE:

WORK — COLOSSIANS 3:23
Whatever you do, work at it with all your heart, as working for the Lord, not for men.

DIGGING DEEPER

I discovered that every Nobody has a Dream, and it's never too late to pursue it! I know you thought your Dream died, but a Big Dream never dies. Your Dream is here somewhere, waiting for you. And if you don't pursue it, something very important won't happen.

— BRUCE WILKINSON, THE DREAM GIVER

1. **Attraction:** Which people group would you enjoy spending time with?	**To get you thinking — a few People Groups:** Professionals College/Young Adults Children Singles Married Couples Families Teens Senior Citizens Disabled Military Personnel Homeless Athletes Internationals Men Women Orphans Other? _____
2. **Needs:** What 1-3 needs are most compelling to you?	**To get you thinking — some Needs:** Environment Healthcare Employment Counseling Housing Finance Education Human Resources Relationships Communications Legal Concerns Personal Development Spiritual Direction/Ministry Safety/Security Other? _____
3. **Talents:** What 1-3 skills do you most enjoy using?	**To get you thinking — various Talents:** Teaching Artistic Expression Organization Administration Financial Planning Creativity Speaking Leadership Carpentry Coaching Music Mechanical Cooking Management Design Sports Hospitality Writing Gardening Photography/Graphic Arts Research Other? _____

4. **Summary:** Combine your Attraction + Needs + Talents in several ways. Brainstorm some ways you might address a need that compels you with people you enjoy while using your talents or skills. For example:

Children + Education + Cooking. → "I could be a dietician in a school or school district."

Athletes + Communications + Photography. → "I could be a sports photographer for a local newspaper or television station."

- I could . . .

- I could . . .

- I could . . .

5. **Achievement of a Lifetime:** What one dream continually crosses your mind? What would you do if you had limitless time and resources and no fear of failing? Is God calling you to this dream? Is now the right time to pursue it?

CHAPTER 6
DECISIONS AND COMMITMENTS

Danielle's problems started out innocently enough: She needed a car. When her husband left her, he took their car, leaving her with no way to get their learning-disabled son to his special care provider. The car dealer was only too happy to lease her a new car, convincing her that she could afford it. Things got worse when she found it in her parking lot a few weeks later with some new dents that she couldn't afford to repair. By the fourth month, she started missing car payments.

In the fifth month she received an official-looking legal document in tiny print from the car dealer. They demanded that she return the car immediately if she couldn't catch up on her payments as well as huge penalties and damage charges. She glanced at the letter, confused and frightened, and tossed it aside. As a follower of Jesus, she knew she should pay her bills. But how could she return the car now? How would she get her son to his school? Two ignored letters later, she found herself accused of car theft and ended up in jail.

Who do you think is to blame for the mess in Danielle's life? Explain.

Danielle had to drop out of high school at seventeen to care for her son. She also can hardly read. How might knowing these additional facts change your perspective (if at all) on the question of who is to blame and what practical steps are needed?

PAUSE 1_EXPLORING WHAT GOD SAYS

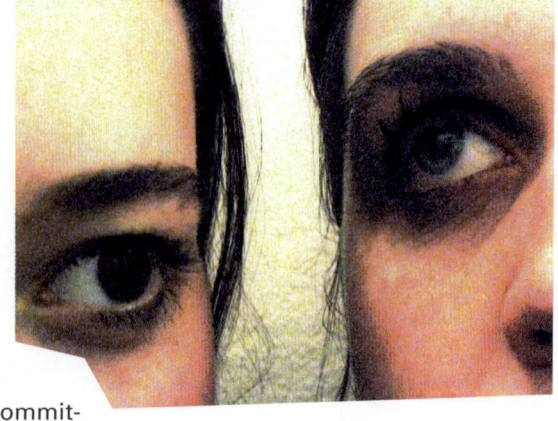

CHOICES. DECISIONS. COMMITMENTS. How do we make the right ones without being random and arbitrary? God wants us to make responsible and ethical choices and keep the commitments we make. But living with the consequences can be tough. That means we have to distinguish between good and evil in our everyday decisions, and then choose to do good, even if it hurts. We know all that. But often it isn't that simple to figure out. In this chapter you will explore the challenges and rewards of making good choices and ethical decisions and then keeping your commitments in a fallen world.

DISTINGUISHING GOOD FROM EVIL

According to these verses, what is one important mark of spiritual maturity?

> *HEBREWS 5:13-14. Anyone who lives on milk, being still an infant, is not acquainted with the teaching about righteousness. But solid food is for the mature, who by constant use have trained themselves to distinguish good from evil.*

God gave us the Ten Commandments to help us tell the difference between right and wrong as a basis for making good decisions. Read prayerfully through the Ten Commandments found in Exodus 20:1-17. What do they reveal about God's heart for people and for society in general?

Now imagine that you are illustrating the Ten Commandments for today's generation. Think about how you see each one being violated. Choose <u>two or three</u> of the commandments and rewrite them below to fit today's realities.

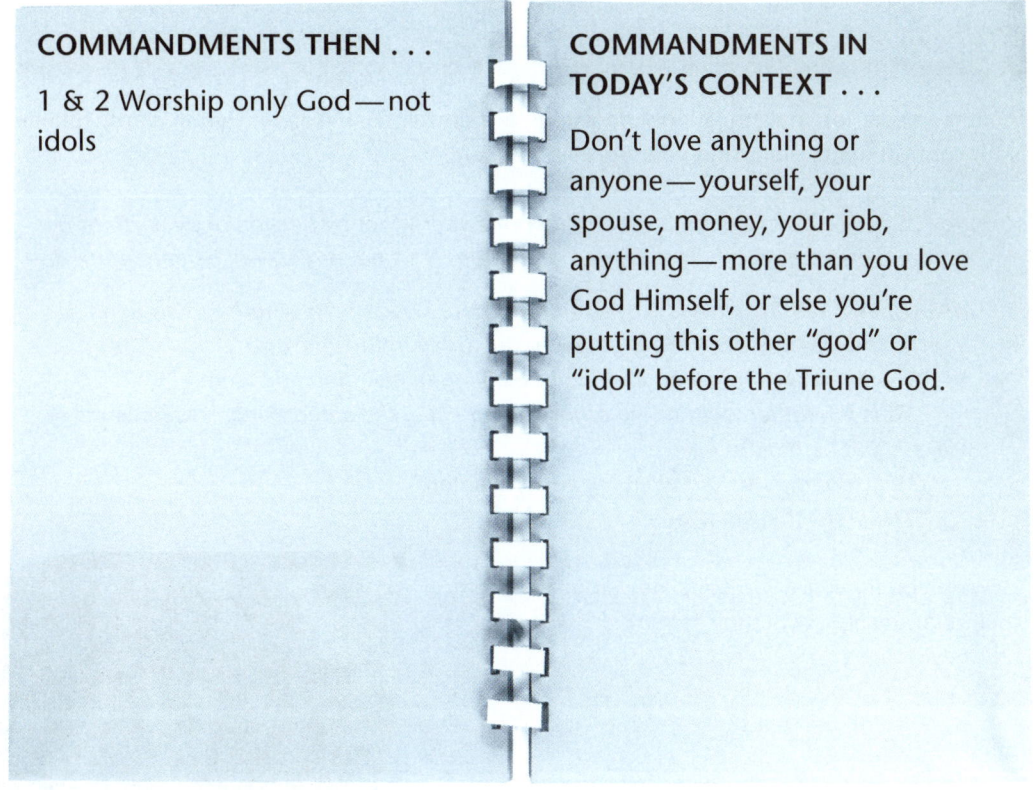

COMMANDMENTS THEN . . .

1 & 2 Worship only God — not idols

COMMANDMENTS IN TODAY'S CONTEXT . . .

Don't love anything or anyone — yourself, your spouse, money, your job, anything — more than you love God Himself, or else you're putting this other "god" or "idol" before the Triune God.

> Ethical *means based on principles of right conduct, moral behavior; virtuous, upright, honorable.*

OWNERSHIP AND FAITHFULNESS

One important basis for making ethical decisions is ownership: honoring what's mine, what's yours, what's ours, what is someone else's — and ultimately what's God's. Can you identify several of the Ten Commandments <u>that protect ownership</u>?

By breaking each commandment you identified, how is someone's right of ownership violated?

> **THINK ABOUT IT . . .**
>
> Did you select the first and second commandments as ones based on ownership? Think about those commandments for a while: no other gods, no idols. God loves us jealously (Exodus 20:5). So He longs for our relationship to be protected from any other things that would steal our hearts away from Him. Since we belong to God, not to ourselves (1 Corinthians 6:19-20), when we have idols in our lives, we violate God's jealous, protective love and His rightful ownership of His creation.

Another basis for making ethical decisions is faithfulness — keeping your word, fulfilling your commitments, honoring your agreements, etc.

> JAMES 5:12. Above all, my brothers, do not swear — not by heaven or by earth or by anything else. Let your "Yes" be yes, and your "No," no, or you will be condemned.
>
> MATTHEW 21:28-31. "What do you think? There was a man who had two sons. He went to the first and said, 'Son, go and work today in the vineyard.'
> "'I will not,' he answered, but later he changed his mind and went.
> "Then the father went to the other son and said the same thing. He answered, 'I will, sir,' but he did not go.
> "Which of the two did what his father wanted?"
> "The first," they answered.

How do you think the two sons' decisions affected their relationships with their father?

Which character in the story are you most like, and why?

In general, is it difficult for you to say "no" to others when you know that answer might hurt or disappoint them? If so, why?

The quiet voice of conscience is drowned out by the cries of the crowd. Evil draws its power from indecision and concern for what other people think.

— BENEDICT XVI, WAY OF THE CROSS

CONSCIENCE

God provides His Holy Spirit, fellow believers, and a conscience to help us make ethical decisions and keep our commitments and promises.

> ACTS 24:16. So I strive always to keep my conscience clear before God and man.
>
> 2 CORINTHIANS 1:12. We can say with confidence and a clear conscience that we have lived with a God-given holiness and sincerity in all our dealings. We have depended on God's grace, not on our own human wisdom. That is how we have conducted ourselves before the world, and especially toward you. (NLT)

What emotions do you feel when you violate your conscience? Do you think feelings of guilt and shame help your spiritual transformation process — or hinder? Explain.

The Holy Spirit also uses our conscience to warn us when we're about to make an unwise decision or a foolish commitment. Has that ever happened to you? Explain.

SUMMARY

Complete these summary statements. We are called:

- To make ethical, right decisions because God is _____ and we're made in His image.
- To keep our commitments and promises because God is _____ and we're made in His image.
- To not worship idols and to keep our marriage vows because God is _____ and we're made in His image.

PAUSE 2_EXPLORING YOUR REALITY

PERSONAL ETHICS SURVEY

As you think about routine ethical decisions you have to make, mark each statement with:

- A for usually Agree
- D for usually Disagree
- NS for Not Sure

____ 1. Pirating software is okay as long as I use it for educational purposes and don't sell it.

____ 2. It's okay to break the code to my online wedding photos and download pictures because I've already paid the photographer for taking them.

____ 3. It's okay to cheat a little on an exam or evaluation to stay competitive.

____ 4. Answering personal e-mail or making personal phone calls at work is okay as long as I keep it to less than an hour a day.

____ 5. It's okay to borrow money and not pay it back if I can't afford to.

____ 6. It's okay to view soft porn because it is only fantasy.

____ 7. It's okay to do whatever seems right to me as long as it doesn't hurt anyone.

____ 8. It's okay to live with my parents or friends without contributing to the rent or household expenses because they love me.

____ 9. It's okay to lie in order to protect the feelings of someone close to me.

____ 10. Another ethical decision I have to make: _____

When you are making decisions, which two or three of the following influence you the most? (Circle whatever applies, and give an example.)

- My personal desires
- Parents
- Friends/Peers
- God's Word
- Conscience
- Mentors
- Media/Movies
- Other?

When you were a child, were promises and commitments made to you usually kept or usually broken? Explain.

> *A person who cannot be depended upon by others, in time, becomes unable to depend upon himself. It seems in some subtle way to undermine and weaken the character when we do not hold ourselves strictly responsible for what we say.*
>
> — LAURA INGALLS WILDER AS QUOTED IN STEPHEN W. HINES, *SAVING GRACES*

What feelings do you have when you imagine making long-term commitments?

What long-term commitments have you made? How are you doing in keeping those commitments, even when it hurts?

CASE STUDY

Do you remember news stories about corporate executives stealing company funds, causing thousands of employees to lose their retirement funds? What about now? Do you recall a recent public scandal where some official or leader was caught doing something unethical or illegal? Discuss the impact this scandal had on society.

Now recall a story about someone you know, or a public official, who made a difficult decision ethically or was faithful to a commitment at great cost to him/herself. What impact did this have on society?

Think about Danielle's story at the beginning of this chapter. Do you think that any public officials or social systems should share any of the blame for Danielle's dilemma or should have stepped in to help her? Why, or why not?

PRAYER PAUSE

When have you been hurt by someone who made an unethical decision or broke a commitment? Take some time to talk with God about any remaining unforgiveness or bitterness in your heart. Ask Him to heal areas of cynicism and mistrust that you still carry as a result of this event. Considering that not keeping commitments is a form of lying, ask God to speak to you about your own decisions and commitments. And thank Him for keeping every single promise He's ever made to anyone — including you.

PAUSE 3_COMING ALIVE TO GOD AND OTHERS

CASE STUDY: OBADIAH AND KING AHAB

CHARACTERS:

- Ahab — one of the most wicked and immoral kings ever to rule in ancient Israel
- Jezebel — Ahab's non-Israelite wife, who worshipped pagan gods and hated God and His prophets
- Obadiah — a devout follower of God who served as Ahab's chief administrator
- Elijah — God's vocal prophet who denounced the evil and obscene practices of the king and queen

Read the story of Obadiah and King Ahab in 1 Kings 16:29-33; 18:1-17. What meaning or purpose do you think Obadiah found in being in charge of an evil king's palace?

What ethical decisions was Obadiah confronted with in his job?

How do you see God using Ahab and Jezebel, as well as Elijah, to help and mature Obadiah?

What type of person might be a modern-day Obadiah?

Can you relate to Obadiah as a worshipper of God employed by an unethical or godless leader? If so, how?

What do these verses say about pleasing people?

> GALATIANS 1:10. Am I now trying to win the approval of men, or of God? Or am I trying to please men? If I were still trying to please men, I would not be a servant of Christ.

> 1 THESSALONIANS 2:4. On the contrary, we speak as men approved by God to be entrusted with the gospel. We are not trying to please men but God, who tests our hearts.

Recall a time when you made an important ethical decision. Try to capture below the messages or pressures you were hearing from various sides. Looking back, do you think you primarily pleased people or God or yourself?

Sometimes making ethical decisions is more about why we do something (our motives and attitude) than it is about exactly what we do. In other words, sometimes we can do the "right" thing for the wrong reasons.

In Pause 1 you explored the Ten Commandments. In His Sermon on the Mount, Jesus revisited many of those commandments and took them to the heart level. His words challenged people to think about their motives and attitudes — not just their final choices. Choose <u>one</u> of these topics to read about:

    MATTHEW 6:1-4.   *Giving to the Needy*
    MATTHEW 6:5-8.   *Praying*
    MATTHEW 6:16-18.   *Fasting*

From the passage you chose, explain how we can do these good things for bad reasons.

Define grace in your own words:

Training to distinguish good from evil is an ongoing part of our spiritual journeys. Of course, nobody gets it right every single time. It takes God's grace for us to succeed — and lots of God's compassion when we fail. God often uses other people to express His grace and mercy to us.

How can you show grace and compassion to those who make decisions you don't think are ethical?

How can you show grace and compassion to yourself when you fall short in similar ways?

Who can support you as you try to live well by pleasing God in your decisions and commitments?

PRAYER PAUSE

Has God reminded you of any commitment or promise that you made to someone but haven't kept? What will you do now to be more faithful? Also talk with Him about the decisions you're facing now, and how you can please Him, not just other people, in the choices you make.

PAUSE 4_JOURNEYING FORWARD

PSALM 94:12. How blessed the man you train, GOD, the woman you instruct in your Word. (MSG)

PSALM 90:12. Oh! Teach us to live well! Teach us to live wisely and well! (MSG)

How have you experienced God this week?

We live in a world of images that deeply influence how we look at life. Choose a picture from this chapter that is meaningful or disturbing to you, and briefly explain why.

Select one verse or insight from this chapter that was meaningful to you this week and write it here.

From your study, respond to one of these questions in the Journal on the following page:

- Through this chapter, what has God shown you about yourself or about Him?
- What has God been saying to you about living life well in decisions and commitments?
- What specific step of action may God want you to take in response to your study?

JOURNAL

SUGGESTED MEMORY VERSE:

DECISIONS AND COMMITMENTS — HEBREWS 5:14

But solid food is for the mature, who by constant use have trained themselves to distinguish good from evil.

DIGGING DEEPER

CASE STUDY: RAHAB

Many ethical decisions are just not a simple matter of "black and white." Here's one story that illustrates how hard it is to live ethically in a "gray" world. Consider how this woman made a decision to honor God, even though she risked her life to do so. Read JOSHUA 2:1-24.

What ethical dilemma(s) was Rahab facing?

How did Rahab's decision impact others, including the two spies, her family, the Israelites, and the people of Jericho?

Although Rahab was a prostitute and she lied to the authorities (verses 1,4-6), she is praised in Hebrews 11:31. Why do you think this is so?

CASE STUDY: PHARMACIST

Now apply the principles from 1 Kings and this whole Bible study to this modern-day case study.
    Not long ago, the Food and Drug Administration approved the "morning after" pill (to end a pregnancy) for over-the-counter sales. Many pro-life pharmacists have ethical concerns about this drug. So the law currently allows pharmacists to refuse to sell this medication if their consciences won't allow them to. Other people challenge this freedom, insisting that pharmacists should be required to issue any drug that is legal for sale.

If you were a pharmacist, what guidelines would help you in making this ethical decision?

CHAPTER 7
AUTHORITY

Claudia despised authority. She enjoyed pushing the limits and knew how to avoid getting caught. It really didn't matter who was in charge. Authority just seemed like a bad idea left over from earlier human history.

Claudia's strong dislike for authority started when she was a kid. Her dad had dominated everyone in the family. She complained that her school teachers squelched her energy and ideas. From the police to higher levels of government, she saw power and authority being abused all over the place.

Now as a follower of Jesus she is noticing her rebellious spirit — which she used to call her "creative" side. And submitting to God's authority seems more like death than the freedom in Christ that attracted her to Him in the first place.

If you were Claudia's friend, what concerns would you have for her?

PAUSE 1_EXPLORING WHAT GOD SAYS

Did you ever wonder where authority and power came from, and how it all started? Well, creation wasn't just about sunsets and flowers and animals and the laws of nature. Everything began with God. He holds ultimate power in the cosmos and created the invisible and visible structures of kingdoms and leadership. The challenge is responding to human authorities as God wants us to for the safety and protection of all of us. In these verses mark <u>anything that is under God's authority</u>.

> DANIEL 7:14. He [the Son of Man] was given authority, honor, and sovereignty over all the nations of the world, so that people of every race and nation and language would obey him. His rule is eternal—it will never end. His kingdom will never be destroyed. (NLT)

> MATTHEW 28:18. Then Jesus came to them and said, "All authority in heaven and on earth has been given to me."

> COLOSSIANS 1:15-16. Christ is the visible image of the invisible God. He existed before anything was created and is supreme over all creation, for through him God created everything in the heavenly realms and on earth. He made the things we can see and the things we can't see—such as thrones, kingdoms, rulers, and authorities in the unseen world. Everything was created through him and for him. (NLT)

Why do you think authority and power were given to Jesus? And what is He doing with His power and authority?

What else has God done with His authority on earth (in addition to sharing it with Christ)?

> ROMANS 13:1-2. Everyone must submit himself to the governing authorities, for there is no authority except that which God has established [placed in power—NLT]. The authorities that exist have been established by God. Consequently, he who rebels against the authority is rebelling against what God has instituted, and those who do so will bring judgment on themselves.

How does it make you feel to know that all human authority — local, national, international — is established by God?

As you read the following verses about leadership and authority,

- Underline how we are to respond
- Circle why we are to respond in those ways

ROMANS 13:3-7. *For the authorities do not strike fear in people who are doing right, but in those who are doing wrong. Would you like to live without fear of the authorities? Do what is right, and they will honor you. The authorities are God's servants, sent for your good. But if you are doing wrong, of course you should be afraid, for they have the power to punish you. They are God's servants, sent for the very purpose of punishing those who do what is wrong. So you must submit to them, not only to avoid punishment, but also to keep a clear conscience.*

⁶ Pay your taxes, too, for these same reasons. For government workers need to be paid. They are serving God in what they do. Give to everyone what you owe them: Pay your taxes and government fees to those who collect them, and give respect and honor to those who are in authority. (NLT)

1 TIMOTHY 2:1-4. *I urge you, first of all, to pray for all people. Ask God to help them; intercede on their behalf, and give thanks for them. Pray this way for kings and all who are in authority so that we can live peaceful and quiet lives marked by godliness and dignity. This is good and pleases God our Savior, who wants everyone to be saved and to understand the truth.* (NLT)

HEBREWS 13:17. *Obey your spiritual leaders and do what they say. Their work is to watch over your souls, and they are accountable to God. Give them reason to do this with joy and not with sorrow. That would certainly not be for your benefit.* (NLT)

2 PETER 2:9-10. *So you see, the Lord knows how to rescue godly people from their trials, even while keeping the wicked under punishment until the day of final judgment. He is especially hard on those who follow their own twisted sexual desire, and who despise authority. These people are proud and arrogant, daring even to scoff at supernatural beings without so much as trembling.* (NLT)

From these verses, what do you think submitting to authority has to do with leading "peaceful and quiet lives marked by godliness and dignity"? (1 Timothy 2:2, NLT)

> *To submit means choosing to come under someone's influence.*
>
> — BILL THRALL, LEADERSHIP CATALYST, INC.

What do you think happens when nobody is in authority? (Judges 21:25; 2:18-19)

For many of us, one hard place to respect leaders and obey authorities is at work. Not many of us work as slaves or household servants anymore. So as you read these verses, it may help you to substitute "employee" or "worker" for "servant" or "slave." Also substitute the words "manager" or "boss" for the word "master." Mark what stands out to you about <u>relating to authorities in work settings</u>.

> 1 PETER 2:18-23. *You who are servants, be good servants to your masters — not just to good masters, but also to bad ones. What counts is that you put up with it for God's sake when you're treated badly for no good reason. There's no particular virtue in accepting punishment that you well deserve. But if you're treated badly for good behavior and continue in spite of it to be a good servant, that is what counts with God.*
>
> *21-25 This is the kind of life you've been invited into, the kind of life Christ lived. He suffered everything that came his way so you would know that it could be done, and also know how to do it, step-by-step. He never did one thing wrong, not once said anything amiss.*
>
> *They called him every name in the book and he said nothing back [he did not threaten revenge (NLT)]. He suffered in silence, content to let God set things right.* (MSG)
>
> EPHESIANS 6:5-9. *Servants, respectfully obey your earthly masters but always with an eye to obeying the real master, Christ. Don't just do what you have to do to get by, but work heartily, as Christ's servants doing what God wants you to do. And work with a smile on your face, always keeping in mind that no matter who happens to be giving the orders, you're really serving God. Good work will get you good pay from the Master, regardless of whether you are slave or free.*
>
> *Masters, it's the same with you. No abuse, please, and no threats. You and your servants are both under the same Master in heaven. He makes no distinction between you and them.* (MSG)

From these passages, if we follow Jesus' example in relating to authorities, what are several things people will see in our lives?

I find it interesting that Jesus never reprimanded His disciples for wanting "to be great." Instead He dramatically redefined the terms of greatness and pointed His disciples in another direction entirely. You can be leaders, He told them, but you must take the route of sacrifice, suffering and service.

— STACY RINEHART, UPSIDEDOWN

In Matthew 20:25-28, what radical concept of leadership did Jesus teach and model for His followers?

What does it mean to "lord it over" someone (verse 25)? Have you experienced or done this?

Is it okay to want to be great? If so, what would that look like in God's eyes?

PAUSE 2_EXPLORING YOUR REALITY

What was your experience of authority in your past: with your parents, relatives, teachers, or other officials? Are there still strong emotions attached to any of those experiences? If so, explain.

What is your general attitude toward authority now (respect, trust, compliance, fear, resistance, suspicion, disgust)? How does your attitude impact the way you relate to authorities?

What authority do your parents have in your life now? Explain.

> If you are having trouble getting along with [authority], you may be having "transference feelings." Transference is when you experience feelings in the present that really belong to some unfinished business in the past. Suppose your supervisor tells you that he wants something done differently. Immediately you feel "put down." You think, He never thinks I do anything right. I'll show him. Your supervisor may have made the comment in passing, but the feelings it triggered were very strong indeed. The reality is that the interaction may be tapping into unresolved hurt from past authority relationships, such as parents or teachers. When a transference relationship starts, you may begin to act out all the old patterns you did with parents. This never works. You become a child on the job.
>
> — HENRY CLOUD AND JOHN TOWNSEND, *BOUNDARIES*

Do you trust that God can and does work on your character through the authorities He places over you? Explain.

Who is currently under your authority? How do you think you are doing in handling your authority properly?

If Jesus sent you a text message about authority, what do you think it might say?

PAUSING TO PRAY

As you pause to pray over your relationships with authorities, let God bring things to your mind. Also invite God to show you if any of your responses to authority have roots in painful or negative experiences in the past. Ask God to forgive you and receive His forgiveness and mercy. Also ask God to show you how to honor and serve people — whether they are under or over you in authority.

PAUSE 3_COMING ALIVE TO GOD AND OTHERS

God is honored when we respect His ultimate authority and the limited authority of human leaders. But it's really tough to respect some leaders. Most of us have known what it feels like to work for a poor boss — or even a terrible boss. Some of us have faced pressure from authorities to do something corrupt, unethical, or illegal. The following story is about choosing to obey the authority of God when it contradicts the authority of man.

CASE STUDY:
SHADRACH, MESHACH, AND ABEDNEGO WITH KING NEBUCHADNEZZAR

> **HISTORICAL BACKGROUND**
>
> *Shadrach, Meshach, and Abednego were friends of Daniel — young Jewish men who were captured when the Babylonian King Nebuchadnezzar conquered Israel. They were sent into exile in Babylon where they faced many ethical challenges throughout their lives. When King Nebuchadnezzar ordered everyone in the land to fall down and worship a huge golden statue, these three men had a life-or-death choice to make: Obey the king and dishonor God, or respectfully disobey the king in order to obey God.*

Read their story in DANIEL 3:12-30.

What ethical dilemma(s) did Shadrach, Meshach, and Abednego face? Imagine Shadrach, Meshach, and Abednego wrestling with this choice: Either obey King Nebuchadnezzar or obey God — but not both. What do you imagine they were feeling and saying to one another?

What impact did their submission and obedience to God have on the heart of King Nebuchadnezzar and the nation of Babylon?

Have you or someone you know had to make a difficult decision when the demands of men conflicted with the ways of God? How did that choice affect others? Explain.

How can we still honor authority even in the rare cases when we know God is calling us to disobey them, as Daniel's friends did?

Scripture has a lot to say to those who have been given spiritual authority or leadership in the church, and to those who follow spiritual leaders. From 1 Peter 5:1-7, what are we told about

- exercising spiritual authority

- following spiritual authorities

Give an example of a spiritual leader you know who showed these positive characteristics. What impact did it have?

What primary character quality does this passage urge us to develop (verses 5-6)? Why do you think that is so important?

How and why did Jesus display humility and submit to authority? (Philippians 2:8)

Mark below how Jesus the Good Shepherd exercises His authority and protection over us.

*PSALM 23:1-3. The L*ORD *is my shepherd, I shall not be in want. He makes me lie down in green pastures, he leads me beside quiet waters, he restores my soul. He guides me in paths of righteousness for his name's sake.*

ISAIAH 40:11. He tends his flock like a shepherd: He gathers the lambs in his arms and carries them close to his heart; he gently leads those that have young.

JOHN 10:14-15. I am the good shepherd; I know my sheep and my sheep know me — just as the Father knows me and I know the Father — and I lay down my life for the sheep.

How does your heart feel about submitting to Jesus' authority in light of these truths?

PAUSE 4_JOURNEYING FORWARD

PSALM 94:12. How blessed the man you train, GOD, the woman you instruct in your Word. (MSG)

PSALM 90:12. Oh! Teach us to live well! Teach us to live wisely and well! (MSG)

How have you experienced God this week?

We live in a world of images that deeply influence how we look at life. Choose a picture from this chapter that is meaningful or disturbing to you, and briefly explain why.

Select one verse or insight from this chapter that was meaningful to you this week and write it here.

From your study, respond to one of these questions in the Journal on the following page:

- Through this chapter, what has God shown you about yourself or about Him?
- What has God been saying to you about living life well in authority?
- What specific step of action may God want you to take in response to your study?

# JOURNAL

SUGGESTED MEMORY VERSE:

AUTHORITY — ROMANS 13:1

Everyone must submit himself to the governing authorities, for there is no authority except that which God has established. The authorities that exist have been established by God.

DIGGING DEEPER

It's a sad fact: Sometimes spiritual leaders misuse their authority. What events in the news have depicted spiritual leaders abusing their authority? Or, have you ever been personally hurt by such a spiritual leader? Explain.

In these passages, how did spiritual leaders abuse their authority?

EZEKIEL 34:1-10

LUKE 11:46

From these passages, how does God feel about those who misuse authority — spiritual and otherwise? And how does He feel toward those who have been hurt by authorities instead of helped?

> *Enemy-occupied territory — that is what this world is.*
> — C. S. LEWIS

Satan and his crew of demons are alive and well![1] For mysterious reasons, God allows Satan to exert influence and have some authority on this earth, although it is illegitimate. But God has ultimate authority in the cosmos and in our lives. He has not left us helpless or powerless before Satan's schemes.

From these passages, how can believers resist evil spiritual authorities in the name of Jesus?

EPHESIANS 6:10-13

2 CORINTHIANS 10:4-6

JAMES 4:7

1 PETER 5:8-9

---

[1] To learn more about resisting the rule of Satan, see chapter 8 in *RELATIONSHIPS: Bringing Jesus into My World* in this series.

Where do you see yourself currently in the ongoing war with evil spiritual authorities?

How do you see submitting to God and resisting the Devil going together in your spiritual journey?

CHAPTER 8
CHURCH

Tim's new job was exciting. But he was lonely in this new city, missing friends and family. He searched for connection — even thought about church. He used to attend with his family. But now that he was on his own he questioned the purpose. Wasn't the church filled with older people and families? Why did he need to attend a formal service in a building? Couldn't he just talk to God in his own way and try to live a good life?

One morning at the coffee shop, Tim read a newspaper article about Andrew, a young businessman (like himself) in Belarus. After the fall of communism, Andrew began seeking God and experienced life transformation. He described how alive he feels when he is enjoying the close community with fellow believers in his city.

But recently the political tide began to shift in Belarus. The new government was suppressing worship of Christ by denying plans for a new church building. Soon Andrew's pastor was thrown into prison for holding worship services on a nearby farm. Andrew wondered if he, too, would be imprisoned for his ongoing ministry with high-school students. He knew that others had died for their faith, and he was willing to go to prison if needed.

Andrew's story really got Tim's attention, even though their church experiences had been so different. Maybe there was community and life connected to local believers. Maybe the same purpose and passion Andrew experienced as part of the body of Christ were available to him. Then it hit him hard: Maybe the persecution that believers were facing in Belarus could come to his town someday.

What gets your attention from Andrew's story — or Tim's? What questions does it raise for you?

PAUSE 1_EXPLORING WHAT GOD SAYS

Have you noticed that romance is "in" these days? You can get matched up online or watch romantic encounters on television. But romance and passion aren't just twenty-first-century ideas. The greatest romance in history isn't found in the media: It is the story of God romancing the Church to be His Son's eternal bride. In this chapter you will explore the true identity of Church, her purposes on earth, and the beauty of her unity and her diversity.

CHURCH AS CHRIST'S BRIDE

When Christ looks at Church, He doesn't see a religious organization or a social institution or a building or any kind of "it." Christ sees His Church as His beloved bride. Highlight anything you notice about Christ's love for His bride the Church.

> *EPHESIANS 5:25-27. Husbands, love your wives, just as Christ loved the church and gave himself up for her to make her holy, cleansing her by the washing with water through the word, and to present her to himself as a radiant church, without stain or wrinkle or any other blemish, but holy and blameless.*
>
> *2 CORINTHIANS 11:2. I am jealous for you with a godly jealousy. I promised you to one husband, to Christ, so that I might present you as a pure virgin to him.*
>
> *REVELATION 21:2. And I saw the holy city, new Jerusalem, coming down out of heaven from God, made ready as a bride adorned for her husband.*
> (NASB)

As you consider being part of the Church, how do you experience Jesus cleaning you up and making you more beautiful?

How do you relate to the idea of being Christ's bride — whether you're a man or a woman? What feelings surface as you imagine yourself as His eternal spouse?

What does this metaphor of Church as bride reveal about the heart of God?

OTHER METAPHORS FOR CHURCH

Here are some other metaphors used in the Bible to describe the Church. Select one of these metaphors for Church (perhaps the one that you connect with the most). Read the verses provided.

THE BODY OF CHRIST	THE TEMPLE/BUILDING OF THE HOLY SPIRIT	THE FAMILY/CHILDREN OF GOD
Romans 12:4-5 Colossians 1:17-18 Ephesians 5:30	Ephesians 2:19-22 1 Corinthians 3:16-17 1 Peter 2:4	John 1:12-13 Romans 8:15-17 2 Corinthians 6:18 Hebrews 2:11-12

Now sum up how you think the Church is like a body, a temple, or a family of sons and daughters.

PURPOSES OF CHURCH

You've already learned that Church exists for the sake of the Bridegroom — so that He will enjoy her presence with Him for eternity in heaven. But beforehand, she has significant purposes to accomplish here on earth. What do you think is another major purpose of the Church in the world today?

FOR ONE ANOTHER

We are included in Church for the sake of one another, as these passages reveal. From these passages, what do you notice about the first followers of Jesus "being there" for each other?

ACTS 2:42-47

HEBREWS 10:23-25

> Confession requires community — the witness of trusted brothers and sisters. . . . Jesus is intent on freeing us to be a fellowship of sinners. He will transform his bride through our exposing our rags to each other rather than concealing them behind gleaming shame coats. . . . We experience confession in the Body of Christ as "that posture of nakedness before God and with others" that leads to our healing. . . . Through confession we become known [by] . . . trustworthy "priests" in our faith communities . . . trustworthy fellow believers who can hear my confession and support me in my recovery.
>
> — ANDREW COMISKEY, STRENGTH IN WEAKNESS

As God transforms us, He often uses other people — both believers and nonbelievers. From your knowledge of the Bible, list as many ways as you can think of that believers are encouraged to come alongside one another. For example, we're told to love one another, carry one another's burdens, etc.

One of the more overlooked "one another's" in the Bible is to confess our sins and struggles to one another. Confessing is coming out of hiddenness into God's light. The purpose isn't to shame us into better behavior, but to experience healing from our shame and forgiveness for our sin. Read ACTS 19:18 and JAMES 5:16 (and the quote by Comiskey above).

Why do you think it is so important for our spiritual journeys for us to confess to a few trusted and grace-filled others — not just to God? Who is there in your church or faith community that you confess your sins and struggles to?

FOR THOSE WHO DON'T YET FOLLOW JESUS[1]

From each passage below, summarize the purposes of Church being in the world.

ISAIAH 49:6

ACTS 1:8

2 CORINTHIANS 5:18-20

REVELATION 22:17

What if those in Christ's Church prepare to be His bride and faithfully love one another, but they don't witness for Him or take His gospel to the ends of the earth and they don't invite those who thirst to the living water that Jesus offers? What impact would that have on the world?

---

[1] For more on "one another," loving others, and those who don't yet follow Jesus, see *RELATIONSHIPS: Bringing Jesus into My World* in this series.

PAUSE 2_EXPLORING YOUR REALITY

Describe where your childhood family was in terms of spirituality and religion. Would you describe your family members as religious or secular or something else?

Do you feel a part of any local church or gathering of the body of Christ in your area? If so, how is your experience with those people impacting your spiritual journey?

How are you impacting others in your church on their spiritual journeys?

Do you see yourself and others playing an important part in the spiritual journeys of your friends, family, and enemies who don't know Jesus yet? If so, how?

What do you think (or feel) about . . .

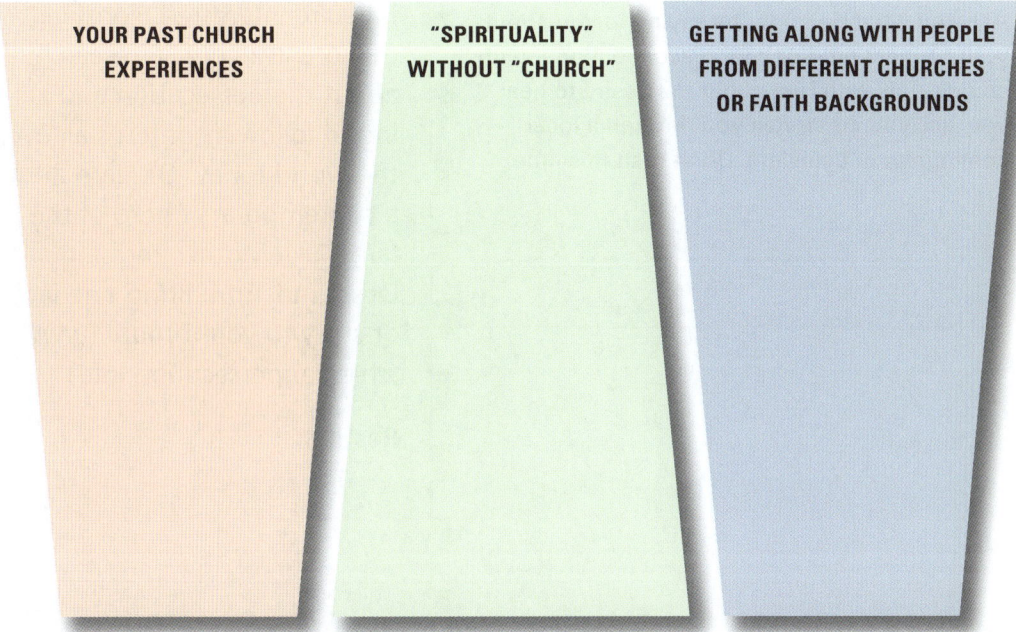

Explain any areas of resistance or pain within you related to a local church or church leader.

As you view the next ten years of your life, how might you like to contribute to Christ's Church? . . . to receive from Christ's Church?

After all you've learned in this study, if a friend asked you, "Why should I become involved in a local church?" what would you say?

PRAYER PAUSE

Ask God what He might be saying to you about your connection — or your disconnection — with church. Talk with Him about His desire to heal you, use you, or stretch you through a local community of believers. Don't rush this time.

Gaining Perspective

If you're interested, consider doing a little online research about the persecution and killing of followers of Jesus all over the world today. Or learn about a contemporary "hero of the faith" like Mother Teresa or Desmund Tutu. Bring one fact or story to your group. (www.christianpersecution.info)

Results:

NOTE: See the Digging Deeper section at the end of this chapter to learn more about the history of the Church. Also note that the kingdom of God is bigger than the sum total of all the local churches and mission efforts (see Revelation 5:9-14). It includes the angels and everywhere God rules. Learn more about the kingdom of God in *RELATIONSHIPS: Bringing Jesus into My World* in the CONNECT Bible study series.

PAUSE 3_COMING ALIVE TO GOD AND OTHERS

UNITY AND DIVERSITY OF CHURCH

Sadly, we in Christ's Church have allowed lots of things to divide us. But much greater things unite us, especially worshipping the Triune God and pursuing the mission of love that He left for us to fulfill. Our unity in Christ's body doesn't mean that we are all alike, or that we agree on everything. Just before He was arrested and crucified, Jesus prayed this to His Father:

> JOHN 17:3,8,18,20-23. Now this is eternal life: that they may know you, the only true God, and Jesus Christ, whom you have sent. . . . They [the Twelve] believed that you sent me. . . . As you sent me into the world, I have sent them into the world. . . . I pray also for those who will believe in me through their message, that all of them may be one, Father, just as you are in me and I am in you. May they also be in us so that the world may believe that you have sent me. . . . May they be brought to complete unity to let the world know that you sent me and have loved them even as you have loved me.

From Jesus' words, what is His Church's purpose in the world, and why do you think our unity is so important for accomplishing that mission?

God created amazing diversity in His natural universe — like over 350,000 different species of beetles! Maybe we shouldn't be so surprised or dismayed that He allows great diversity in His Church, too. One way to think of this diversity is by picturing six broad traditions or great "streams" of faith flowing across the centuries. Each major tradition tends to emphasize a different aspect of walking with Christ, but, of course, believers from each tradition practice the other aspects, too, while worshipping and serving Him. They partially explain why we have different denominations today.

FAITH EXPRESSIONS	PRIMARY CONTRIBUTIONS
Contemplative	a life filled with **PRAYER** and **SILENCE**
Social Justice	a life moved by **COMPASSION** and **SERVICE**
Evangelical	a life centered on proclaiming **SCRIPTURE**
Charismatic	a life empowered by **THE HOLY SPIRIT**
Holiness	a life characterized by **VIRTUE***
Sacramental	a life of experiencing God through **SACRAMENTS****

— Adapted from Richard Foster, *Streams of Living Water*

* Virtue means "moral excellence, righteousness, or goodness."
** Sacraments are "visible expressions of God's invisible grace, like baptism and holy communion."

Which one or two of these expressions of faith (if any) do you identify with in your own spiritual journey? Explain.

How might other traditions of church benefit your journey with Jesus?

The apostles pioneered going to places where there were no local churches and the gospel wasn't known (see Acts 13). God still calls people from local churches to launch new gospel initiatives, or into specialized ministries to meet special needs. Parachurch organizations such as World Vision and The Navigators may specialize in feeding the hungry, starting hospitals, or living among those in military communities or university campuses in order to advance the gospel.

Have you benefited from any specialized ministries? Or do you sense God calling you to become involved in a pioneering or specialized ministry? Explain.

HEROES OF THE FAITH

HEBREWS 11:32–12:1 gives us a partial list of the heroes of the faith mentioned in the Bible. As you read about them, jot down below what they accomplished and endured for the sake of Christ.

What they accomplished:

What they endured:

Besides these men and women, who is on your personal "heroes of the faith" list?

Now it is our turn to be Church. One day our names will be on this amazing list. How do you feel about the way we are running our race (12:1)?

DESTINY OF THE CHURCH

On earth the Church is busy creating community, experiencing transformation, and accomplishing her mission. But in heaven these activities will fade away as we focus on our one eternal calling: to worship and enjoy God forever.

> *PHILIPPIANS 2:10-11. That at the name of Jesus every knee should bow, in heaven and on earth and under the earth, and every tongue confess that Jesus Christ is Lord, to the glory of God the Father.*
>
> *REVELATION 5:9. And they sang a new song: "You are worthy to take the scroll and to open its seals, because you were slain, and with your blood you purchased men for God from every tribe and language and people and nation."*

REVELATION 22:1-5. Then the angel showed me the river of the water of life, as clear as crystal, flowing from the throne of God and of the Lamb down the middle of the great street of the city. On each side of the river stood the tree of life, bearing twelve crops of fruit, yielding its fruit every month. And the leaves of the tree are for the healing of the nations. No longer will there be any curse. The throne of God and of the Lamb will be in the city, and his servants will serve him. They will see his face, and his name will be on their foreheads. There will be no more night. They will not need the light of a lamp or the light of the sun, for the Lord God will give them light. And they will reign for ever and ever.

Respond to these visionary verses about the Church's destiny any way you want to — in song, with a drawing, in prayer, on your knees — whatever you feel like.

PRAYER PAUSE FOR THE CHURCH

Close your time of study in prayer for the Church all over the world, as well as for any local churches you are connected to. Perhaps pray for persecuted believers, for church leaders, and for those wounded by church leaders. Also ask God to accomplish His mission through His Church of reaching and discipling others while living out the ways of Jesus.

Lord . . . help us to aid our neighbors in need, even when this interferes with our own plans and desires. Help us to realize that it is a grace to be able to share the cross of others and, in this way, to know that we are walking with you along the way. Help us to appreciate with joy that when we share in your suffering and the sufferings of this world, we become servants of salvation and are able to help build up your Body, the Church.

— BENEDICT XVI, *WAY OF THE CROSS*

PAUSE 4_JOURNEYING FORWARD

PSALM 94:12. How blessed the man you train, GOD, the woman you instruct in your Word. (MSG)

PSALM 90:12. Oh! Teach us to live well! Teach us to live wisely and well! (MSG)

How have you experienced God this week?

We live in a world of images that deeply influence how we look at life. Choose a picture from this chapter that is meaningful or disturbing to you, and briefly explain why.

Select one verse or insight from this chapter that was meaningful to you this week and write it here.

From your study, respond to one of these questions in the Journal on the following page:
- Through this chapter, what has God shown you about yourself or about Him?
- What has God been saying to you about living life well in church?
- What specific step of action may God want you to take in response to your study?

# JOURNAL

SUGGESTED MEMORY VERSE:

CHURCH — EPHESIANS 5:25-27

Christ loved the church and gave himself up for her to make her holy, cleansing her by the washing with water through the word, and to present her to himself as a radiant church, without stain or wrinkle or any other blemish, but holy and blameless.

DIGGING DEEPER_JOURNEY OF THE CHURCH

Life-giving community breeds life-giving followers. . . . The early churches had a way of allowing the Holy Spirit to spend them on the horizontal by serving and loving, while simultaneously having their own lives transformed on the vertical, through worship and study. That's the way of the Cross; to go and make disciples while we continue to apprentice ourselves to the Master Jesus.

— ERIC SANDRAS, BUCK-NAKED FAITH

Luke carefully recorded the story of the early church in the book of Acts. There we can discover how the early church was organized, what disagreements and struggles they experienced, and what forms they used to fulfill the core functions and purposes of the church. He also described some of the astonishing ways God helped the early church to flourish despite severe government oppression and persecution of believers, both of which continue even today in many places.

Read as many of these selected passages from the book of Acts as you want to. Record your thoughts in the chart below as you go. We'll get you started with a few observations.

___ 2:40-47 ___ 7:54–8:1 ___ 15:5-21
___ 4:31-35 ___ 11:19-30 ___ 15:36-41
___ 5:12-16 ___ 13:1-3 ___ 16:1-5
___ 6:1-7 ___ 15:1-4 ___ 17:1-15

How was the early church organized? 2:46 — met in homes	**What disagreements and struggles did they have?** 7:54–8:1 — persecution & martyrdom
What were some of the activities and forms they used? (e.g., worship, love) 6:1-7 — cared for widows & distributed food	**What were some of the core purposes they fulfilled?** 2:41 — baptism & other sacraments
How did God help the early church to flourish? 11:21 — God's hand was with them, so many believed	**Other observations:**

THE JOURNEY OF THE CHURCH

So what has happened to the Church since Christ ascended into heaven? How did we get from the small, dynamic home groups of the first century to the massive institutions and hundreds of denominations and sects in the twenty-first century? How has the gospel spread around the world? Maybe this very brief snapshot will help.

EARLY CHURCH

AROUND AD 29

The Church of Jesus began in Israel. After He was crucified, His disciples spread the church throughout the Roman world, northern Africa, and into India. In Antioch followers of Jesus were first called "Christians." The society didn't recognize churches as legitimate. They struggled and they thrived. They served with love and they lived out the gospel in difficult times. Eventually regional church centers grew up across the Mediterranean area in Jerusalem, Antioch, Rome, Alexandria, and Constantinople. They had a dominating influence in the doctrines and practices of the Church in the first few centuries AD.

THE FIRST MARTYRS

An early Christian historian named Tertullian said, "The blood of the martyrs is the seed of the church." That is because thousands of the earliest Christians accepted death rather than renounce their faith in Christ. Stephen was the first Christian martyr mentioned in the Bible (Acts 6:8-8:1). Tradition tells us that most of the original twelve disciples were killed because of their commitment to Christ. Under the Roman Empire, thousands of Christians who refused to betray Christ were fed to lions as a form of "entertainment" for Roman crowds. They paid a huge price for obeying Jesus and sharing in His suffering.

THE CHURCH GETS ORGANIZED

AD 313

In AD 313 Emperor Constantine recognized Christianity as one of various official religions in the Roman Empire, substantially ending the persecution of Christians for that time. Then in AD 380 Christianity was made the official religion by Emperor Theodosius. The Roman Catholic Church was born in 452 led by Pope Leo the Great. This organizing of the church allowed more freedom to believers and also opened the church to those who were less committed to the ways of Jesus.

THE CHURCH DIVIDES

By AD 1054 the church in Rome and the other regional centers divided over the issue of icons (religious art). Politics and language also contributed to this division that had brewed for many years. The Roman Catholic Church and the Eastern Orthodox Church came to form the two major divisions within the church. Meanwhile the church in India and elsewhere continued without much interaction with these major branches.

THE PROTESTANT REFORMATION

Many people inside the Roman Catholic Church objected to some practices that were abuses of New Testament teachings, and they tried to reform the church. In AD 1517, Martin Luther, a reformer from Germany, published a paper protesting many abuses in the church. This helped spark the Protestant Reformation. A major result of the Reformation was bringing the Bible to the masses. Now ordinary people could read the Scriptures for themselves and draw their own conclusions. Over time this reformation has resulted in the formation of thousands of Protestant denominations and mission efforts, reflecting diverse traditions and expressions of the Christian faith.

MISSIONARY MOVEMENTS

From Acts in the first century until today, church missions has always been going on. These apostolic efforts complemented the work of local churches. Missions usually tried to reach out to those who would not hear the gospel within their ordinary contexts. Meanwhile local churches often focused on building up and caring for those who believed and reaching out to those who were close by.

Sometimes these missionary or apostolic movements were fueled by the persecution of the church. The faith and love of martyrs often drew others to faith in Jesus. At other times, the institutional church aligned itself with political agendas of the day and tried to expand the kingdom of God through the sword and power of governments. The Crusades and European colonization are sad examples of the church turning from the ways of the Cross and of love to the ways of human power and violence. Some missionaries opposed the colonial agenda. They tried to maintain the integrity of the gospel message while contextualizing it into the customs and cultures of the people.

Around 1793 William Carey began what has been called the Modern Missionary Movement. He believed that the gospel was intended for all people. So Carey moved from England to India, translated the Bible, established hospitals, and preached the gospel to many.

THE CHURCH TODAY

Today the church is both expanding and contracting. In China, Korea, Africa, India, and South America, many people are turning to follow Jesus, especially through house churches. In much of Europe, Canada, and the United States, the church is diminishing both in size and in influence. In modern centuries, states have abused their ties to the church. So the pendulum has swung in the opposite direction from the Middle Ages, with laws in place to separate the church from the state.

CURRENT PERSECUTIONS AND MARTYRS

In each period of church history, men and women have offered costly acts of love and sacrifice in the name of Jesus. Most people don't realize how widely Christians are being persecuted around the world today. More heroes of the faith have suffered or died for their faith in Christ during the twentieth and twenty-first centuries than in any previous century. The majority of modern-day persecution occurs in the "10-40 window." The 10-40 window refers to countries that are located between the 10th and the 40th geographical parallels on a world map. Many of the poorest countries and most of the unreached peoples of the world live there, including most of the world's Muslims, Hindus, and Buddhists.

THE FUTURE OF THE CHURCH

Christ's Church is not static. God is moving history closer and closer to the time of Christ's return, even though nobody knows exactly when this will happen. What we do know is that the future of the Church is absolutely secure. The Bridegroom will return for His bride, the Church.

As you reflect on this very brief overview of the history of the Church, what is:

- one interesting thing you have learned?

- one question you still have?

- one headline you would predict for the church in the next fifty years?

RESOURCE: *If you're interested in learning more about the fascinating history of Jesus' followers, here are two good places to start:* Church History in Plain Language *by Bruce L. Shelley (Nelson, 1996) and* A Short History of Christianity *by Stephen Tomkins (Eerdmans, 2006).*

CHAPTER 9
GLOBAL ISSUES

Terrell and LaTanya are anxious. Should they have children or not? The prospect of raising a child in a world of terror feels very scary. Diseases, wars, suicide bombers, economic uncertainty, global warming, flu pandemics, sexual predators . . . all reported instantly so every bad thing happening nearby and far away is in your face every day. Who wants their kids to grow up in such an uncertain mess? And besides . . . isn't Jesus coming back soon?

Do you think about global issues a little or a lot? What feelings do you have as you consider these issues? Explain.

The world is shrinking. Well, not physically. But our planet is becoming one big global village in a lot of ways. The Internet, media, and airline industries whiz information and people around the globe in nanoseconds and hours instead of days and weeks. But all this interconnectedness brings dangers right to our doorstep, too — such as deadly diseases and images of terrorism and war. And actual acts of terrorism and war aren't far behind. In this chapter we'll explore how followers of Jesus can connect with global concerns.

PAUSE 1_EXPLORING WHAT GOD SAYS

An important place to begin is to remember that humanity's story is part of God's story. And He has given us glimpses into the future.

Study **Matthew 24** as Jesus describes the "end of the age." To help you understand this astounding story, we've divided it into four parts. At the end of each brief section, sum up its highlights in three or four sentences.

    MATTHEW 24:1-14   **Birth Pains**

    MATTHEW 24:15-28   **The Antichrist**

    MATTHEW 24:29-37   **The Return of Christ**

    MATTHEW 24:38-41   **The Time Unknown**

Most movies and literature about the end of the world depict planet earth and civilization as "dying." Why do you think Jesus describes this period of time as "birth pains"? (verse 8)

What do you see in current events that indicates increasing hostility toward followers of Christ? How do you feel about the possibility of you being persecuted for your faith in your lifetime? (verse 9)

What do you think will make the difference between those who are deceived and those who are not? (verses 5,11)

Pause a moment to think about the sobering fact that most people's love for Christ will grow cold. How is the uncertainty and wickedness of the world around you impacting your love for Christ? (verse 12)

How do you see the gospel of Jesus and His kingdom being preached throughout the world now? (verse 14)

Jesus urges us to be ready for His return. How is being "ready" different from being "fearful"? (verses 42-43)

Do you believe the return of Christ will be in your lifetime? Whichever way you answered, how (if at all) does your belief about Christ's return impact the way you live now?

List here anything you're still worried or confused about from Jesus' words. Bring them to your group for discussion.

-

-

-

PAUSE 2_EXPLORING YOUR REALITY

What major changes in the world do you anticipate might happen within the next twenty-five years?

What emotions surface as you consider living in our world during the next twenty-five years?

If you have children now (or are considering having children later on), how do you feel about bringing children into this uncertain world?

What influence has terrorism had on your thoughts or feelings or choices?

The Old Testament is filled with stories of men and women called by God into positions of political influence. Some handled their authority well (Joseph and Daniel) and many others didn't (Saul). Do you think God still uses people in politics to further His purposes? Explain, and give examples.

PAUSE 3_COMING ALIVE TO GOD AND OTHERS

ENVIRONMENT

One significant global issue is the environment. Pollution, extinction of species, global warming — these issues flood the news and impact the future of humanity and the ecosystem. Notice what the Bible says about nature and the environment.

> GENESIS 1:28; 2:15. *God blessed them and said to them, "Be fruitful and increase in number; fill the earth and subdue it. Rule over the fish of the sea and the birds of the air and over every living creature that moves on the ground." . . . The LORD God took the man and put him in the Garden of Eden to work it and take care of it.*

> ROMANS 8:18-23. *Yet what we suffer now is nothing compared to the glory he will reveal to us later. For all creation is waiting eagerly for that future day when God will reveal who his children really are. Against its will, all creation was subjected to God's curse. But with eager hope, the creation looks forward to the day when it will join God's children in glorious freedom from death and decay. For we know that all creation has been groaning as in the pains of childbirth right up to the present time. And we believers also groan, even though we have the Holy Spirit within us as a foretaste of future glory, for we long for our bodies to be released from sin and suffering. We, too, wait with eager hope for the day when God will give us our full rights as his adopted children, including the new bodies he has promised us.*

> REVELATION 11:18. *The nations were angry; and your wrath has come. The time has come for judging the dead, and for rewarding your servants the prophets and your saints and those who reverence your name, both small and great — and for destroying those who destroy the earth.*

How do you feel about the current state of the global environment? Of your local environment?

Why is it important to protect and care for the environment?

What are your environmental concerns, and what is your part in them?

THE RISE AND FALL OF NATIONS

A whole generation has grown up not knowing a day of peace. In Somalia, for example, more than half of all the children under age five who were alive on January 1, 1992, were dead due to violence by December 31 of that year. The vortex of violence in which the children are trapped becomes even more horrific when we realize how many of them are now involved as soldiers in the front lines themselves — literally hundreds of thousands.

— CAROL BELLAMY, *THE STATE OF THE WORLD'S CHILDREN*

Have you ever wondered why nations succeed and fail over time? Read EZEKIEL 28:1-10,16-22 about the city of Tyre and its king and the neighboring city of Sidon. As you read this account, write down some things about them that led to their downfall.

What part does God play in the rise and fall of nations?

Do you observe any of these dynamics in your nation or other nations? If so, explain.

According to 2 Chronicles 7:14, the healing of global issues begins inside of us. How can we contribute to healing our land?

Does God's ultimate judgment of individuals and nations give you hope — or fear — or something else? Explain.

> Some in the United States judge our nation's success by such measures as gross national product, military might, and global dominance. The kingdom of God measure such things as care for the downtrodden and love for enemies. . . . In that final reckoning, God judges nations by how they treat the poor, the sick, the hungry, the alien, and the prisoner.
>
> — PHILIP YANCEY, *FINDING GOD IN UNEXPECTED PLACES*

How do you imagine God will judge our country when He considers how we "treat the poor, the sick, the hungry, the alien, and the prisoner"? Explain. (See Philip Yancey quote above.)

MIXING OF CULTURES AND SPIRITUALITIES[1]

God delights in diversity in nature and in human culture. And He obviously has allowed freedom for different religions and spiritualities to emerge within those cultures. But we also know that most wars are fought over differences in nationality, economics, ethnicity, and religion that we humans just can't seem to resolve peacefully. Consider below how God dealt with the mixing of cultures and spiritualities at the beginning of mankind's history (Genesis 11) and at the coming end of time as we know it (Revelation 5).

> GENESIS 11:1-9. *At one time all the people of the world spoke the same language and used the same words. As the people migrated to the east, they found a plain in the land of Babylonia and settled there.*
>
> [3] *They began saying to each other, "Let's make bricks and harden them with fire." (In this region bricks were used instead of stone, and tar was used for mortar.) Then they said, "Come, let's build a great city for ourselves with a tower that reaches into the sky. This will make us famous and keep us from being scattered all over the world."*
>
> [5] *But the LORD came down to look at the city and the tower the people were building. "Look!" he said. "The people are united, and they all speak the same language. After this, nothing they set out to do will be impossible for them! Come, let's go down and confuse the people with different languages. Then they won't be able to understand each other."*

---

[1] If you want to explore this topic more, see the Digging Deeper section at the end of the chapter.

⁸ In that way, the LORD scattered them all over the world, and they stopped building the city. That is why the city was called Babel, because that is where the LORD confused the people with different languages. In this way he scattered them all over the world. (NLT)

From Genesis 11:1-9 above, how and why did God diversify and scatter the peoples of the earth?

Now look at God's plan for unifying the people of the earth. Mark whatever stands out to you.

EPHESIANS 2:14-18. For Christ himself has brought peace to us. He united Jews and Gentiles into one people when, in his own body on the cross, he broke down the wall of hostility that separated us. He did this by ending the system of law with its commandments and regulations. He made peace between Jews and Gentiles by creating in himself one new people from the two groups. Together as one body, Christ reconciled both groups to God by means of his death on the cross, and our hostility toward each other was put to death.

¹⁷ He brought this Good News of peace to you Gentiles who were far away from him, and peace to the Jews who were near. Now all of us can come to the Father through the same Holy Spirit because of what Christ has done for us. (NLT)

REVELATION 5:9-10. And they [saints from all the earth] sang a new song: "You are worthy to take the scroll and to open its seals, because you were slain, and with your blood you purchased men for God from every tribe and language and people and nation. You have made them to be a kingdom and priests to serve our God, and they will reign on the earth."

What challenges are you aware of that we face because of the mixing of cultures and religions?

How do you maintain your bearings when everything else in your culture is moving and shifting around you?

Why and how is God uniting the diverse peoples of the earth?

HOPE IN THE MIDST OF UNCERTAINTY

So instead of loving what you think is peace, love other men and love God above all. And instead of hating the people you think are warmakers, hate the appetites and the disorder in your own soul, which are the causes of war.

— THOMAS MERTON, *NEW SEEDS OF CONTEMPLATION*

There are many other global issues not discussed in this chapter, such as: poor nations becoming poorer in the global economy, HIV and Hepatitis C epidemics, genetic manipulation, stem cell research, immigration, drug trafficking, racial conflicts, genocide, slavery, etc. Without Christ, we have every reason to be terrified of the future. But in Christ, we have many reasons for hope.

Lots of external factors contribute to global problems and issues. But this passage points to a primary cause of virtually all the problems you've studied in this chapter. What is that cause?

> JAMES 4:1-3. *Where do you think all these appalling wars and quarrels come from? Do you think they just happen? Think again. They come about because you want your own way, and fight for it deep inside yourselves. You lust for what you don't have and are willing to kill to get it. You want what isn't yours and will risk violence to get your hands on it. You wouldn't think of just asking God for it, would you? And why not? Because you know you'd be asking for what you have no right to. You're spoiled children, each wanting your own way.* (MSG)

What do these passages offer to help us live hopefully right now in the midst of serious global concerns?

PSALM 33:20-22

PSALM 4:8

What do these passages reveal about our ultimate future in heaven?

REVELATION 21:1-8

REVELATION 22:3-6

From everything you have studied, what glimpses of hope do you see in Scripture that will help you face these serious global issues?

Is this really hopeful for you? Explain.

PRAYER PAUSE

Spend some extended time alone with God in prayer and silence. Share with Him your fears, concerns, or desires for the future. Rest in His presence. Ask Him to reveal how He wants you to engage in global issues.

PAUSE 4_JOURNEYING FORWARD

PSALM 94:12. How blessed the man you train, GOD, the woman you instruct in your Word. (MSG)

PSALM 90:12. Oh! Teach us to live well! Teach us to live wisely and well! (MSG)

How have you experienced God this week?

We live in a world of images that deeply influence how we look at life. Choose a picture from this chapter that is meaningful or disturbing to you, and briefly explain why.

Select one verse or insight from this chapter that was meaningful to you this week and write it here.

From your study, respond to one of these questions in the Journal on the following page:
- Through this chapter, what has God shown you about yourself or about Him?
- What has God been saying to you about global issues?
- What specific step of action may God want you to take in response to your study?

JOURNAL

SUGGESTED MEMORY VERSE:

GLOBAL ISSUES — MATTHEW 24:12-13

Because of the increase of wickedness, the love of most will grow cold, but he who stands firm to the end will be saved.

DIGGING DEEPER

There are many different kinds of spirituality to choose from — more than we can count. Some of us sample several belief systems before we come to trust Christ. Others of us grew up in the church and feel very uncomfortable around people from other faith backgrounds. Either way, we're all on a journey. That understanding should help us relate to others on their journeys and communicate our faith in a pluralistic spiritual world with less arrogance. We need to love those whose first step toward the One Triune God is to believe He is the "King above all gods" (Psalm 95:3).

A PERSPECTIVE ON OTHER SPIRITUALITIES

We live in a world of spiritual pluralism. God has allowed a lot of different perspectives on spirituality to exist, and so our spiritual journey may involve choosing one. The Triune God doesn't force us to choose Him.[2] In our global society, why are there so many different views of spirituality? How can reasonable people across the planet come to such different conclusions about spirituality? Maybe it depends on how we view what's "beyond us" out there. We might ask ourselves, "If I stepped outside myself and looked back, what would I conclude? Where would I step? Who lives in this beyond? What does this say about who I am?" All this may seem very confusing and philosophical. It is! Across cultures, humanity has agreed that something exists beyond us (even if it's an illusion of our minds). We just haven't agreed upon what that something beyond us is! Here's what spirituality might look like if we look at it from differing views of "what's beyond us."

- If there is nothing beyond me, if my mind is ultimately all there is, then I may conclude that I am an atheist, or that I am a god or goddess. If I conclude that even my mind is an illusion, then all pursuit of life is a meaningless game, including all spiritualities.
- If my primary point of reference in life is society, if society is the primary force shaping human life, then I may believe there is no God. Or I may doubt His existence or involvement in human affairs. I am essentially a humanist.
- If nature is my point of reference beyond me, then animism may be my belief system. Objects and animal spiritualism may provide sources of inspiration and strength for me.
- If the universe (or multiple universes) is what's beyond, then I may conclude that the universe is alive and is god. This pantheist belief defines me as a force within the broader life force of the universe. I may conclude I am a god or goddess. Or I may conclude that life is an accident generated by a godless universe.

---

[2] See *GOD: Connecting with His Outrageous Love* in this series to explore foundational issues between you and God.

- If the universe was created (in other words, the universe didn't always exist), then I may believe in good and bad gods (polytheism and/or Satanism) or in one God (monotheism). Most of the world's population believes in one or more gods. And the goodness of those gods is questionable.
- If humanity reflects the image of God and humans are relational beings, then I may believe in the paradox of the Trinity, the Three-in-One God.

So with all of these options, how can we know what is real? In the end, we must choose to trust someone whom we believe is trustworthy. That may be the Triune God, a person in authority, our culture, or it may be ourselves alone. The choice is ours.

The journey of spiritual transformation always requires trust. The Triune God built a trust system when He created the universe. God always calls us to choose to trust. If we refuse to trust God, we'll probably end up trusting ourselves. Spirituality is relational. That makes it primarily a question of who is trustworthy enough for us to trust. Every kind of spirituality offers its reasons for believing. But ultimately God has wired humanity to engage in trust with our hearts, minds, bodies, and souls. Though we can't eliminate all doubt as we look beyond, we can choose to trust "someone" who is trustworthy.

Of course, this is just a brushstroke over a complex and mysterious question. But it may help us gain some understanding of how reasonable people can form such different spiritual perspectives.

This exploration of different spiritualities may not be where you are today. You may have concluded that part of your journey, or it may be ahead of you. Either way, we will always share this planet with people who don't trust what we trust and don't doubt what we doubt. Our prayer is that this Digging Deeper can serve as a bridge both for dialogue and for extending the love of Jesus to those whose perspectives are different from ours. We hope that in time they, too, will behold and trust the Triune God who is "the great God, the great King above all gods" (Psalm 95:3).

What strikes you most from this article?

Whom are you able to find trustworthy?

What questions might you still have?

CHAPTER 10
LIFETIME JOURNEY

Once upon a time there was a gray-haired caterpillar named Yellow. One day Yellow happened to meet another caterpillar who told her about becoming a butterfly. "But how do you become one?" she asked.

"You must want to fly so much that you are willing to give up being a caterpillar," he said.

"You mean to die?" asked Yellow.

"Yes and no," he answered. "What <u>looks like you</u> will die, but what's <u>really you</u> will still live."[1]

Think about what caterpillars have to go through to become butterflies. How is our process of spiritual transformation like a butterfly's?

Who determines "what's really you"? Explain.

As we experience God each day, we are being transformed into the image of Christ. Often we experience His goodness through His practical guidance, fierce protection, sweet blessings, or flashes of joy. But God sometimes leads us into dark, cocoon-like places where we may lose any sense of His presence. And yet He uses even those places to transform us and draw us ever closer to Himself. This chapter is about looking at your overall journey, assessing where you are now, and taking purposeful steps into the future.

---

[1] Trina Paulus, *Hope for the Flowers* (Mahwah, NJ: Paulist Press, 1973), 75.

PAUSE 1_EXPLORING WHAT GOD SAYS

> *The contrast between God's way of doing things and our way is never more acute than in this area of human change and transformation. We focus on specific actions; God focuses on us. We work from the outside in; God works from the inside out. We try; God transforms.*
>
> — RICHARD FOSTER, *DEVOTIONAL CLASSICS*

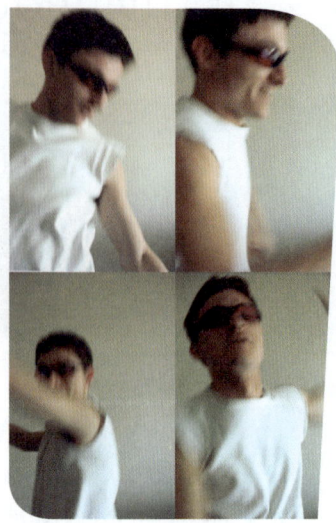

It is very hard to capture in words what it's like to experience spiritual transformation. So hard, in fact, that the Bible uses metaphors to describe the deep changes of transformation and compares them to other kinds of changes in the world around us. Like a vine and branch producing fruit . . . like a seed sprouting green shoots . . . like running a race. And it takes a lifetime. It's an adventure full of ups and downs but ultimately giving life and fulfilling dreams.

> JOHN 10:10. *I came so they can have real and eternal life, more and better life than they ever dreamed of.* (MSG)

In the process of your spiritual transformation, when is a time you've been enthralled with God or you've experienced God's presence or provision in a special way?

LIKE A BRANCH

Have you ever wondered what your relationship with Jesus will look like a little bit farther down the road as you mature spiritually? Jesus compared us to branches bearing fruit. As you read Jesus' words in John 15:5-17, write on the chart below what you observe about:

- What God has done for us
- What Jesus asks of us
- The results of obeying Him

WHAT HAS GOD DONE FOR US?	WHAT HAS JESUS ASKED OF US?	RESULTS
v. 9 Loved us	v. 5 Remain in Him	v. 5 Bear fruit

Read verses 5-8 from John 15 again. What do you think it means for us to "bear fruit"? And what does that have to do with "living well"?

What do you think it looks like to "remain/abide" in Him or to "be joined/connected" with Him?

> I felt . . . an anxiety, a loneliness, and a need for connection with someone. If no connection came, I would start to say things like "Life really stinks. Why is it always so hard? It's never going to change. . . . Who cares? Life is really a joke." Surprisingly, I noticed by the time I was saying those last sentences, I was feeling better. The anxiety was greatly diminished.
> My "comforter," my abiding place, was cynicism and rebellion. From this abiding place, I would feel free to use some soul cocaine — a violence video with maybe a little sexual titillation thrown in, perhaps having a little more alcohol with a meal than I might normally drink — things that would allow me to feel better for just a little while. I had always thought of these things as just bad habits. I began to see that they were much more; they were spiritual abiding places that were my comforters and friends in a very spiritual way; literally, other lovers.
> — BRENT CURTIS AND JOHN ELDREDGE, THE SACRED ROMANCE

In light of this quote, when you are not joined to Jesus or abiding in Jesus, where are you abiding? Explain.

How can you intentionally practice "remaining" or "abiding" in Him this week?

Ask other members in your group what fruit they've seen in you during your transformation process.

LIKE A SEED

At other times when Jesus described life with Him, He used the metaphor of a seed, and the paradox of dying in order to come alive.

> JOHN 12:23-25. Jesus replied, "Now the time has come for the Son of Man to enter into his glory. I tell you the truth, unless a kernel of wheat is planted in the soil and dies, it remains alone. But its death will produce many new kernels — a plentiful harvest of new lives. Those who love their life in this world will lose it. Those who care nothing for their life in this world will keep it for eternity." (NLT)

How was Jesus' life like a seed?

What would it look like for you to live like a seed in this season of your life?

> If you lose your life for my sake, you will find it, Jesus said (Matt. 10:39). Die and become. Could that be the fundamental theme of the New Testament?
>
> — SUE MONK KIDD, WHEN THE HEART WAITS

In your current life season, are you seeing some outward fruit of new life, or is the seed still hidden and growing? Are you experiencing joy, or is it still on the way to the surface? Explain.

> When you're waiting, you're not doing nothing. You're doing the most important something there is. You're allowing your soul to grow up. If you can't be still and wait, you can't become what God created you to be.
>
> — SUE MONK KIDD, WHEN THE HEART WAITS

REALITY CHECK

Whether you are rapidly growing and bearing much fruit, or quietly waiting as a seed sprouts underground, Jesus is lovingly and patiently committed to being with you through all stages of your transformation.

LIKE A RACE

A race is another metaphor to describe what our relationship with Jesus looks like as we mature in our spiritual journey. Underline or highlight some traits of someone moving forward spiritually.

1 CORINTHIANS 9:24-27. In a race, everyone runs but only one person gets first prize. So run your race to win. To win the contest you must deny yourselves many things that would keep you from doing your best. An athlete goes to all this trouble just to win a blue ribbon or a silver cup, but we do it for a heavenly reward that never disappears. So I run straight to the goal with purpose in every step. I fight to win. I'm not just shadow-boxing or playing around. Like an athlete I punish [discipline — NLT] my body, treating it roughly, training it to do what it should, not what it wants to. Otherwise I fear that after enlisting others for the race, I myself might be declared unfit and ordered to stand aside. (TLB)

HEBREWS 12:1-3. Therefore, since we are surrounded by such a great cloud of witnesses, let us throw off everything that hinders and the sin that so easily entangles, and let us run with perseverance the race marked out for us. Let us fix our eyes on [and look away from all that will distract us from — AMP] Jesus, the author and perfecter of our faith, who for the joy set before him endured the cross, scorning its shame, and sat down at the right hand of the throne of God. Consider him who endured such opposition from sinful men, so that you will not grow weary and lose heart.

HEBREWS 12:2 describes Jesus as "the author . . . originator . . . pioneer . . . source" of our faith. What does that mean in terms of your spiritual journey?

The same verse also describes Jesus as "the perfecter . . . finisher . . . completer" of our faith. How does this encourage you in your spiritual journey?

When you think of your spiritual journey now, can you relate more to the metaphor of the branch or the seed or the race or some other metaphor? Explain.

In what important ways do we all need each other in Christ's body to run our races together? (Hebrews 10:24-25; Colossians 3:12-13,16)

We all know that getting in shape physically and staying that way takes regular discipline — kicking our couch-potato habits and engaging in healthy habits. Maturing spiritually will take no less. What spiritual habits or disciplines do you think will help you on your lifetime journey of spiritual transformation? (For more on spiritual habits that help build our relationship with God, see the Digging Deeper section at the end of this chapter.)

PRAYER PAUSE

Talk to God about your journey of spiritual transformation so far. Share your current experiences and feelings. Thank Him for the areas of hope and joy He has brought to your life. Talk with Him about the areas you are still trusting and depending upon Him to complete and make whole. And be frank about the areas you still feel hopeless or anxious or angry about. Thank Him for His ongoing work and unfailing love in your life.

PAUSE 2_COMING ALIVE TO GOD AND OTHERS

To move deeply into the heart of God requires that we move and that God carries us all at the same time. Sure, there are lots of things we can change by sheer willpower — but spiritual transformation is much deeper, as deep as our hearts, minds, and behaviors — as deep as our very soul identity. And of course we'll fall short time after time after time with our proud hearts, broken relationships, persistent addictions, pet sins, and shabby substitutes for real life in Christ. The process is often messy; we may take a few steps forward and then a few steps back. But Jesus and His people also walk with us every step of the way.

SEASONS IN THE JOURNEY

Our spiritual transformation is like a journey and also like a roller-coaster ride, filled with ups and downs, twists and turns. Read the following passage and <u>circle the words that best represent the season you are experiencing now</u> on your transformation journey.

ECCLESIASTES 3:1-8
There is a time for everything,
    and a season for every activity under heaven:
a time to be born and a time to die,
    a time to plant and a time to uproot,
a time to kill and a time to heal,
    a time to tear down and a time to build,
a time to weep and a time to laugh,
    a time to mourn and a time to dance,
a time to scatter stones and a time to gather them,
    a time to embrace and a time to refrain,
a time to search and a time to give up,
    a time to keep and a time to throw away,
a time to tear and a time to mend,
    a time to be silent and a time to speak,
a time to love and a time to hate,
    a time for war and a time for peace.

Think of a previous season in your life. What did you learn about yourself and God in that season?

Think of your life as a book God is writing, and this season is one chapter. What title would you give to this season of your life?

> We can fill ourselves with our own thoughts, ideas, images, and feelings. . . . But if we invite God with our attention, opening the inner spaces with silence, he will speak to our souls, not in words or concepts, but in the mysterious way that love expresses itself — by presence.
>
> — M. BASIL PENNINGTON, *CENTERED LIVING*

How are you experiencing (or not experiencing) God's loving presence during this season of your life?

THE WINTER OF OUR TRANSFORMATION JOURNEY

If we could choose, most of us would choose only experiences of "healing, dancing, laughing, embracing," etc. But, frankly, God also uses times of "tearing, hating, war, and weeping" (Ecclesiastes 3) in order to complete us in His image. For example, Jesus had to go through an agonizing season of betrayal, mockery, beating, abandonment, and death to become our Savior.

Does the list in Ecclesiastes 3 make you aware of something you are avoiding or anxious about? If so, what is it and why are you anxious about it?

How would you want others in your community to help you through the more difficult seasons of your transformation process and to see hope and meaning in the darkness? How have you helped others through their difficult seasons?

Read Philippians 3:10-11. We want to share in the power of Christ's resurrection. But why do you think we also have to share in His suffering?

When the fullness of time comes, a sacred voice at the heart of us cries out, shaking the old foundations. It draws us into a turbulence that forces us to confront our deepest issues. It's as if some inner, divine grace seeks our growth and becoming and will plunge us, if need be, into a cauldron that seethes with questions and voices we would just as soon not hear. One way or another, the false roles, identities, and illusions spill over the sides of our lives, and we're forced to stand in the chaos.

— SUE MONK KIDD, *WHEN THE HEART WAITS*

Most of us want our spiritual journeys to go smoothly. But our reality is often messy, sometimes stagnant, or even chaotic. Have you ever "stood in your own chaos" and recognized that it is an important part of your spiritual journey? Explain.

Sometimes we fear that we'll lose control of our lives if we surrender to God's transforming work in our lives. From this passage, is the result of our spiritual transformation more freedom — or less freedom? Explain.

> *2 CORINTHIANS 3:17-18. Now the Lord is the Spirit, and where the Spirit of the Lord is, there is freedom. And we, who with unveiled faces all reflect the Lord's glory, are being transformed into his likeness with ever-increasing glory, which comes from the Lord, who is the Spirit.*

Have you experienced freedom in your spiritual transformation process? If so, how? If not, how would you like to experience freedom?

The writer of Ecclesiastes concludes his description of the seasons of life with these words:

> ECCLESIASTES 3:11-12; 12:13-14
> He [God] has made everything beautiful in its time.
> > He has also set eternity in the hearts of men;
> > yet they cannot fathom what God has done from beginning to end.
> I know that there is nothing better for men than to be happy and do good while they live.
>
> ¹³ Now all has been heard; here is the conclusion of the matter:
> > Fear God and keep his commandments, for this is the whole duty of man.
> For God will bring every deed into judgment,
> > including every hidden thing, whether it is good or evil.

What one thought from this passage encourages you right where you are now on your spiritual journey? Explain.

HOPE FOR THE JOURNEY

Much about the future really is uncertain, or even feels threatening. In these verses, mark anything that <u>we can be certain of</u> for the rest of our lives — no matter what happens.

> 1 JOHN 3:1-3. How great is the love the Father has lavished on us, that we should be called children of God! And that is what we are! The reason the world does not know us is that it did not know him. Dear friends, now we are children of God, and what we will be has not yet been made known. But we know that when he appears, we shall be like him, for we shall see him as he is. Everyone who has this hope in him purifies himself, just as he is pure.
>
> JEREMIAH 29:11. "For I know the plans I have for you," declares the LORD, "plans to prosper you and not to harm you, plans to give you hope and a future."
>
> PHILIPPIANS 1:6. Being confident of this, that he who began a good work in you will carry it on to completion until the day of Christ Jesus.

How do these passages give you hope or encouragement that God will meet you on your transformation journey?

PAUSE 3_EXPLORING YOUR REALITY

Wonderful, Wild, and Worshipful

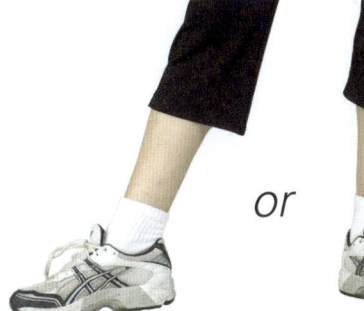

or boring, bland, *and* benign

If you could choose three words to describe your journey of spiritual transformation so far, what would they be?

_____, _____, and _____

How has Jesus met you so far along your spiritual journey?

How has the Holy Spirit empowered you in your spiritual journey?

In the opening story, the butterfly explained "transformation" to the caterpillar this way: "What looks like you will die, but what's really you will still live." In your journey of transformation so far, how have you experienced this?

Transformation occurs within the context of relationships — not all by ourselves. Who are some people who have been spiritual companions or mentors to you on your journey?

Spiritual transformation is not about just trying harder, or performing better. When have you experienced God's provision, presence, and joy as a result of surrender and humility? When are you tempted to be self-sufficient and independent?

What does this passage tell us about how to live unwisely and how to live well in all the areas of our lives?

LIVING UNWISELY			LIVING WELL
	EPHESIANS 5:15-17. Look carefully then how you walk! Live purposefully and worthily and accurately, not as the unwise and witless, but as wise (sensible, intelligent people), making the very most of the time [buying up each opportunity], because the days are evil. Therefore do not be vague and thoughtless and foolish, but understanding and firmly grasping what the will of the Lord is. (AMP)		

Go back to page 12 at the beginning of this study. Read Richard Foster's dream about seeing Jesus' followers living life wisely and well. When you dream about your own life, what are some ways you hope to live well?

- How to _____ well.

- How to _____ well.

- How to _____ well.

- How to _____ well.

SUMMARY THOUGHTS

In this study we've chosen several important areas that will help us become successful in life, like Time, Money, Beauty, Body, Work, and so forth. In the other studies in the CONNECT Bible study series you can explore other areas where Jesus helps us live life well, such as Relationships, Marriage, Sexuality, and Identity. And there are others that will become integrated into your life along your journey. As we are being transformed, it means we are learning to live out key issues of life well as a whole being. Remember that you're not just trying to "manage" your life well. You're inviting God to change and transform you from the inside out. Living life well is the practical outworking of maturing and being transformed inwardly by His Spirit.

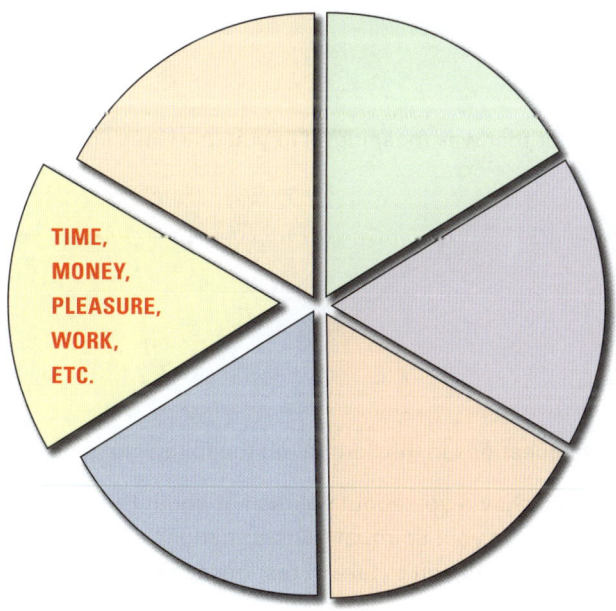

In addition to the topics you've studied in this series, what other aspects of life do you long to mature in and experience Jesus' transforming touch? Write them on the chart.

What lifelong commitment(s) have you made (or do you want to make) about your spiritual transformation journey?

PAUSE 4_JOURNEYING FORWARD

PSALM 94:12. How blessed the man you train, GOD, the woman you instruct in your Word. (MSG)

PSALM 90:12. Oh! Teach us to live well! Teach us to live wisely and well! (MSG)

How have you experienced God this week?

We live in a world of images that deeply influence how we look at life. Choose a picture from this chapter that is meaningful or disturbing to you, and briefly explain why.

Select one verse or insight from this chapter that was meaningful to you this week and write it here.

From your study, respond to one of these questions in the Journal on the following page:

- Through this chapter, what has God shown you about yourself or about Him?
- What has God been saying to you about your spiritual transformation?
- What specific step of action may God want you to take in response to your study?

JOURNAL

SUGGESTED MEMORY VERSE:

SPIRITUAL TRANSFORMATION — PHILIPPIANS 1:6

Being confident of this, that he who began a good work in you will carry it on to completion until the day of Christ Jesus.

DIGGING DEEPER

SPIRITUAL HABITS FOR LIFE

> HEBREWS 12:2. *Let us fix our eyes on Jesus, the author and perfecter of our faith, who for the joy set before him endured the cross, scorning its shame, and sat down at the right hand of the throne of God.*

Our spiritual transformation is more a by-product of beholding God and becoming enthralled with Christ than it is about what we do or don't do. In this last chapter of the entire CONNECT series, we continue to focus on how we can "fix our eyes" on Jesus in the process of our spiritual transformation.

We could learn from people who are farther down the road on their journeys. Down through the ages, the men and women who have enjoyed deep intimacy with God are those who "seriously engaged in a fairly standard list of disciplines for the spiritual life. . . . A small number of [spiritual disciplines] are absolutely central to spiritual growth. They must form a part of the foundation of our whole-life plan for growth as apprentices of Jesus. These are, on the side of abstinence — solitude and silence, and on the side of positive engagement — study and worship." (Dallas Willard, *The Divine Conspiracy*)

Spiritual disciplines or habits usually fall into one of two kinds. The habits of abstinence invite us to stop doing some ordinary things for a while. They help us shift our gaze away from things that would distract us from Jesus. By themselves they are not bad things. It's just that they can clog up our interior landscapes and create such background noise in our souls that we can't hear His gentle and quiet voice. They include temporarily pursuing:

Solitude   (fasting from the presence of other people in person, Internet, media, etc.)
Silence   (fasting from noise)
Fasting   (fasting from food or other things)
Frugality (fasting from spending)
Sacrifice (fasting from keeping things for ourselves)

The habits of engagement invite us to do some things that will help us actively focus our attention on God and His kingdom for a while. Of course practicing them doesn't win God's favor — we already have that! They do help us connect with God and experience His grace and truth as we notice things we've avoided or couldn't see before. They include:

Bible Study	Service	Confession
Worship	Prayer	Scripture Meditation
Celebration	Fellowship	Giving

Which habit of walking with Christ and fixing your eyes on Him will you seek to maintain over the next six months or so? (See *SOUL: Embracing My Sexuality and Emotions*, chapter 10, in this series for more ideas on beholding God.)

> *The secret [of the sweet, satisfying companionship] of the Lord have they who fear (revere and worship) Him, and He will show them His covenant and reveal to them its [deep, inner] meaning.*
>
> — PSALM 25:14 (AMP)

CELEBRATING YOUR GROUP

Somewhere deep down, we know that if we are to survive we must come together and rediscover ways to connect with each other, and with the earth that supports our collective life. We are social beings who need one another not just for physical survival but also for spiritual sustenance as we journey together. So our individuality only makes sense in the context of community, where we are free to become ourselves.

— JONATHAN S. CAMPBELL WITH JENNIFER CAMPBELL, *THE WAY OF JESUS*

As you and your group finish this study, it's a good time to celebrate together. Your relationships have deepened through these past weeks. You've learned much from each other — truths, joys, pains. So we encourage you to plan a celebration. Take some time to "Reflect Back," "Envision Forward," and "Pause to Affirm and Pray."

REFLECT BACK

Share how you've benefited from studying God's Word with this group of fellow spiritual journeyers.

How has your walk with God been affected?

How has your daily lifestyle changed?

What emotions surface as you reflect on your times together?

ENVISION FORWARD

What are your spiritual needs as you consider the next phase of your journey?

In what environment might these needs be met?

What continuing relationships will you have with the people in this group (casual friendship to in-depth involvement)?

Are there other people you know who could benefit from studying this series?

Would one or more people from this group facilitate a new group? Is God leading anyone to be a part of a new group?

PAUSE TO AFFIRM

Do you want to express a thank you or affirmation to anyone in the group who has influenced your life? Take time to do that.

PAUSE TO PRAY

Spend time together praying. Thank God for this part of your journey. Praise Him for who He is. Linger longer together.

WHY MEMORIZE SCRIPTURE?

You won't find the word *memorize* in the Bible. But the concept is there both in command and in example ("treasure . . . store up . . . hide" God's words in our hearts). We are encouraged to "study . . . reflect on . . . delight in . . . not forget" God's words (Psalm 119:9-16, NLT; 37:31).

- "lay hold of . . . pay attention . . . listen closely . . . keep [God's words] within your heart" (Proverbs 4:4,20-22).
- "bind them [my commands] around your neck . . . write them on the tablet of your heart" (Proverbs 3:3).
- "always treasure my commands. . . . Guard my instructions as you guard your own eyes. Tie them on your fingers as a reminder. . . . Write them on the tablet of your heart" (Proverbs 7:1-3, NLT, NIV).
- "it is good to keep these sayings in your heart" (Proverbs 22:18, NLT).
- "meditate on [God's words] day and night" (Joshua 1:8).

These same verses also explain the reasons for and benefits of memorizing Scripture:

- "that I might not sin against you . . . [my] feet do not slip" (Psalm 119:9-16; 37:31).
- "they bring life . . . and healing to their whole body" (Proverbs 4:22, NLT).
- "find favor with both God and people . . . earn a good reputation" (Proverbs 3:3-4, NLT).
- "you will trust in the Lord" (Proverbs 22:18-19, NLT).
- "you will be sure to obey everything written in it. Only then will you prosper and succeed" (Joshua 1:8, NLT).
- so that you'll "have all of them ready on your lips" (Proverbs 22:18).
- "your words . . . were my joy and my heart's delight" (Jeremiah 15:16).

Perhaps even more compelling than these reasons is seeing how powerfully God can use a person who has taken the time and effort to consistently memorize Scripture. When Jesus faced Satan (see Matthew 4:1-11), He drew from the many verses of Scripture that He had memorized in His youth to pinpoint Satan's deception and resist temptation. Where would we be if Jesus had not memorized Scripture? When Peter addressed the huge crowd on the day of Pentecost, he was given no time to consult his concordance and prepare a message! Because he had made Scripture memory a priority in his life, he could quote from three different Old Testament passages that helped bring three thousand people to the Lord!

If you long to equip yourself to counteract Satan, resist sin, trust and obey God, listen to God's voice, and minister to others, there is no better investment of your time than memorizing Scripture.

A good place to begin is by revisiting the verses you memorized here in this study. Carry the verses around. Put them on your PDA. Put them on your computer. Review them out loud. Often. Write them out until you can say them accurately. Meditate on them. Pray over them. Tell a friend what they mean to you. Put yourself to sleep at night thinking about them. And look forward to listening to God speak to you!

I am amazed at the countless times God pulled from my mind a memorized verse that has been exactly the right thing at the right time! At times it was a comfort, at times guidance. A push ahead or a pull to stop. A reminder of His promise, a prompting for wisdom. A word for counseling another, an insight for those seeking our Lord.

— DENNIS STOKES

SCRIPTURE MEMORY VERSES

TIME
EPHESIANS 5:15-16
Be very careful, then, how you live — not as unwise but as wise, making the most of every opportunity, because the days are evil.

MONEY
1 TIMOTHY 6:17
Command those who are rich in this present world not to be arrogant nor to put their hope in wealth, which is so uncertain, but to put their hope in God, who richly provides us with everything for our enjoyment.

BEAUTY AND PLEASURE
PSALM 16:11
You have made known to me the path of life; you will fill me with joy in your presence, with eternal pleasures at your right hand.

MY BODY
1 CORINTHIANS 6:19-20
Don't you realize that your body is the temple of the Holy Spirit, who lives in you and was given to you by God? You do not belong to yourself, for God bought you with a high price. So you must honor God with your body. (NLT)

WORK
COLOSSIANS 3:23
Whatever you do, work at it with all your heart, as working for the Lord, not for men.

DECISIONS AND COMMITMENTS
HEBREWS 5:14
But solid food is for the mature, who by constant use have trained themselves to distinguish good from evil.

AUTHORITY
ROMANS 13:1
Everyone must submit himself to the governing authorities, for there is no authority except that which God has established. The authorities that exist have been established by God.

CHURCH
EPHESIANS 5:25-27
Christ loved the church and gave himself up for her to make her holy, cleansing her by the washing with water through the word, and to present her to himself as a radiant church, without stain or wrinkle or any other blemish, but holy and blameless.

GLOBAL ISSUES
MATTHEW 24:12-13
Because of the increase of wickedness, the love of most will grow cold, but he who stands firm to the end will be saved.

LIFETIME JOURNEY
PHILIPPIANS 1:6
Being confident of this, that he who began a good work in you will carry it on to completion until the day of Christ Jesus.

CONNECT SERIES OVERVIEW

CONNECT is designed to help you discover and embrace the truth Jesus spoke of in a holistic way. We long to see you enjoying life as a member of God's kingdom and family, deeply experiencing His presence, knowing His truth, resting in His love, and confident in His hope. These studies are designed to be used in small groups where people can encourage, trust, and support each other on their spiritual journeys.

CONNECT is arranged as a series of studies. These studies will present foundational biblical principles for primary relationships in life. Jesus summed up what life is all about when He said, "'Love the Lord your God with all your heart and with all your soul and with all your mind.' This is the first and greatest commandment. And the second is like it: 'Love your neighbor as yourself'" (Matthew 22:37-39). Growing in your love for God, for others, and for yourself while managing your personal life in ways that honor Him — now that is a real spiritual journey!

In case this is your first experience in the CONNECT series — or even if you have journeyed through other studies before you picked up this one — this overview may help you connect some dots.

GOD: Connecting with His Outrageous Love is about receiving God's love and loving Him in response.

IDENTITY: Becoming Who God Says I Am and *SOUL: Embracing My Sexuality and Emotions* are about discovering who God says we are and learning to live out of that true identity.

RELATIONSHIPS: Bringing Jesus into My World is about loving people — all kinds of people. Because if we're loving God and ourselves, then loving people will happen naturally.

LIFE: Thriving in a Complex World is about living life well with Jesus. You'll see these themes unfold if you study them in order. But they may also be studied individually or in any order.

Our prayer is that we all will grow in deeper intimacy with God from a heart of worship as we humbly follow Jesus' ways, truth, and life!

ABOUT THE AUTHORS

RALPH ENNIS is the Director of Intercultural Training and Development for The Navigators. Ralph and his wife, Jennifer, have ministered with The Navigators since 1975 in a variety of areas, including at Norfolk military bases, Princeton University, Richmond Community, Glen Eyrie Leadership Development Institute, and with The CoMission in Moscow, Russia. Ralph has a master's degree in Intercultural Relations. Some of his publications include *Searching the Ordinary for Meaning; Breakthru: Discover Your Spiritual Gifts and Primary Roles; Successfit: Decision Making Preferences; An Introduction to the Russian Soul;* and *The Issue of Shame in Reaching People for Christ.*

Ralph and Jennifer currently live in Raleigh, North Carolina. They have four married children and nine grandchildren.

REBECCA GOLDSTONE is a National Training Team consultant for The Navigators. Before joining The Navigators, Rebecca was a consulting partner with The Navigators in training and developing The CoMission project staff and leaders from the former Soviet countries. After leaving The CoMission Rebecca pioneered and developed a crosscultural urban ministry in Santa Ana, California. She is a training consultant, life coach, and serves on the faculty of Hope International University. Her role on the National Training Team consists of creating and editing resources related to spiritual transformation and strategic tools to equip leaders ministering to the millennial generation.

Rebecca and her husband, Marc, live in Irvine, California. They have two children, Ryan and Joshua.

JUDY GOMOLL is Director of School Agreements as a National Training Team Associate. Before joining The Navigators, Judy was an educator with a specialty in curriculum development. Judy and her husband, George, served with The Navigators as missionaries in Uganda and Kenya for fifteen years, where they helped pioneer ministries in communities, churches, and at Makerere University. Judy led in leader training and designing of contextualized discipleship materials and methods. In her current role with the National Training Team, Judy is assisting in the research, development, and field testing of spiritual transformation training tools and resources. She also directs our partnerships agreements with seminaries and graduate schools.

Judy has a master's degree in Curriculum and Instruction, and in Organizational Leadership. She and George live in Parker, Colorado.

DENNIS STOKES has been serving with The Navigators since 1973. During that time he has ministered on collegiate staff, as well as being a collegiate trainer and national training consultant. Dennis has designed, developed, and led seven summer training programs for The Navigators, and was the training coordinator for the CoMission project to the former Soviet Union. He is ordained and speaks at training events, conferences, and in church pulpits in the United States and twelve different countries. He also leads and participates on numerous training teams. In his role as the National Training Director for the U.S. Navigators, Dennis leads out in strategic planning, leading, and implementing national initiatives for staff training and development.

Dennis and his wife, Ellen, live in Erie, Colorado, and have three children — Christopher, Cheryl, and Amy.

CHRISTINE WEDDLE is Associate Director of National Training and Staff Development and has been on staff with The Navigators since 1997. She first connected with The Navigators when she joined the CoMission Training Team. In this role she assisted in the planning and organization of staff training events in the United States, Russia, and the Ukraine.

Since moving to Colorado Springs in 1998, she has directed numerous national training and staff development events. She specializes in developing adult learning environments and visual resources.

Connect Even More!

The CONNECT series is designed to help you discover and embrace the truth Jesus spoke of in a holistic way. By using the series in a small group, you will find encouragement, trust, and support from others as you travel together on this spiritual journey.

God: Connecting with His Outrageous Love
Ralph Ennis, Judy Gomoll, Dennis Stokes, Christine Weddle
978-1-60006-258-2
1-60006-258-X

This study presents a foundational biblical principle for primary relationships in life: receiving God's love and loving Him in response.

Identity: Becoming Who God Says I Am
Ralph Ennis, Judy Gomoll, Dennis Stokes, Christine Weddle
978-1-60006-259-9
1-60006-259-8

Discover who God says you are and learn to live out your true identity by loving God, others, and yourself.

Soul: Embracing My Sexuality and Emotions
Ralph Ennis, Judy Gomoll, Rebecca Goldstone, Dennis Stokes, Christine Weddle
978-1-60006-262-9
1-60006-262-8

Find out how growing in your love for God, for others, and for yourself will help manage your personal life in ways that honor Him.

Relationships: Bringing Jesus into My World
Ralph Ennis, Judy Gomoll, Rebecca Goldstone, Dennis Stokes, Christine Weddle
9-781-60006-261-2
1-60006-261-X

Receiving God's love and in turn loving others is God's plan for us. But loving others as ourselves is not always easy. Learn how to reach out in love to family, friends, and others who may be more difficult to love.

To order copies, call NavPress at 1-800-366-7788, or log on to www.navpress.com.